Oxford English Picture Dictionary

E C Parnwell

illustrated by Ray and Corinne Burrows

Oxford University Press

How to use this Picture Dictionary

To find the English word for something, look through the Contents list, and decide which picture page is likely to show the word you want. The objects will be found in their natural groups—for example, all animals will be found on the pages headed **Animals** and on the page headed **On the Farm**. When you turn to the pictures, you will see that all the animals have numbers beside them. Look for those numbers underneath each picture. The English names for the animals will be beside them.

When you have found the word you are looking for, try to learn some of the other words on the same page. Then cover all the words up and see how many you can remember.

In the Index beginning on page 82 you will find a list of all the English words in this dictionary in alphabetical order. These words are followed by phonetic symbols to help you learn how to pronounce them, and also by two numbers, e.g. **26**/3. The first number tells you what page the object is on and the second tells you which object the word refers to.

Oxford University Press, Walton Street, Oxford OX2 6DP

Oxford New York Toronto Madrid
Delhi Bombay Calcutta Madras Karachi
Kuala Lumpur Singapore Hong Kong Tokyo
Nairobi Dar es Salaam Cape Town
Melbourne Auckland
and associated companies in
Berlin Ibadan

OXFORD and OXFORD ENGLISH
are trade marks of Oxford University Press

ISBN 0 19 431160 0 (limp edition)
© Oxford University Press 1977
First published 1977
Eighteenth impression 1992

Printed in Hong Kong

Contents

4 Our Universe
5 The World
8 The Human Body
10 Clothes
14 In Town
16 The Law
17 Fire and Medical Services
18 Education
20 In the Supermarket
21 In an Office
22 At the Post Office
23 On a Building Site
24 In a Workshop
25 Tools
26 A House
27 The Weather/In the Garden
28 The Hall
29 The Sitting-room/Living-room
30 The Kitchen
31 Household Objects
32 The Bedroom/The Baby
33 The Bathroom and Toilet
34 In the Country

35 By the Sea
36 On the Farm
37 Power
38 Travel
45 National Defence
46 Recreation
53 Sewing
54 Occupations/Professions
56 Animals
61 Plants
64 Verbs
67 Containers
68 Lines and Shapes
69 Measurement
70 Time, Date, Temperature
71 Family Relationships
72 Nouns of Quantity
74 Adjectives
76 Prepositions
79 Colours
80 Numbers Weights and Measures
81 Pronunciation and Stress
82 Index

A. In Space
1 comet
2 constellation
3 galaxy
4 planet
5 star
6 Moon
7 Earth
8 Sun
9 orbit

B. Phases of the Moon
10 eclipse

11 new/crescent moon
12 half moon
13 full moon
14 old moon

C. Space-travel
15 nosecone
16 rocket
17 launching-pad
18 satellite
19 (space-)capsule
20 astronaut
21 spacesuit

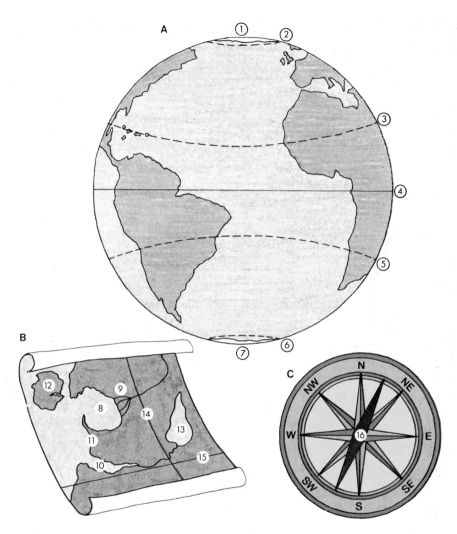

A. Globe
1 North Pole
2 Arctic Circle
3 Tropic of Cancer
4 Equator
5 Tropic of Capricorn
6 Antarctic Circle
7 South Pole

B. Map
 8 bay
 9 delta
10 estuary
11 coastline
12 island

13 lake
14 line of longitude
15 line of latitude

C. Compass
16 needle
   N   north
   NE northeast
   E   east
   SE southeast
   S   south
   SW southwest
   W   west
   NW northwest

A. Continents
1 North America
2 South America
3 Europe
4 Africa
5 Asia
6 Australia
7 Antarctica

B. Oceans
8 Arctic
9 North Pacific
10 South Pacific
11 North Atlantic
12 South Atlantic
13 Indian
14 Southern/Antarctic

C. Seas, Gulfs, Bays
15 Gulf of Alaska
16 Hudson Bay
17 Gulf of Mexico
18 Caribbean Sea
19 Gulf of Guinea
20 North Sea
21 Baltic Sea
22 Mediterranean Sea
23 Black Sea
24 Caspian Sea
25 Red Sea
26 Persian Gulf
27 Arabian Sea
28 Bay of Bengal
29 Coral Sea
30 Tasman Sea

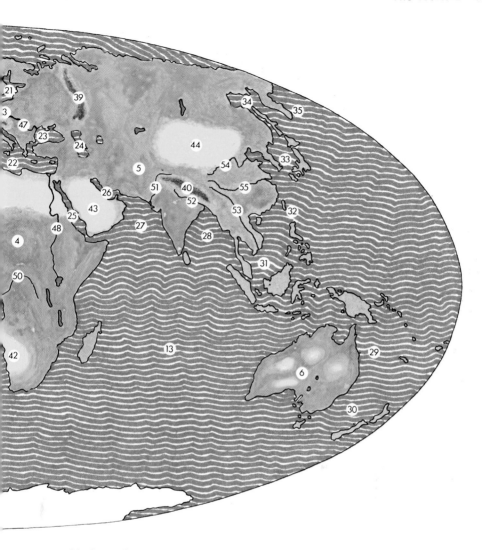

31 South China Sea
32 East China Sea
33 Sea of Japan
34 Sea of Okhotsk
35 Bering Sea

D. Mountain Ranges
36 Rockies
37 Andes
38 Alps
39 Urals
40 Himalayas

E. Deserts
41 Sahara
42 Kalahari
43 Arabian
44 Gobi

F. Rivers
45 Mississippi
46 Amazon
47 Danube
48 Nile
49 Niger
50 Congo
51 Indus
52 Ganges
53 Mekong
54 Huang He (Yellow)
55 Yangtze

A

B

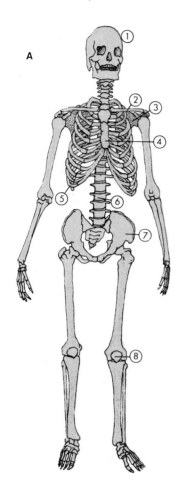

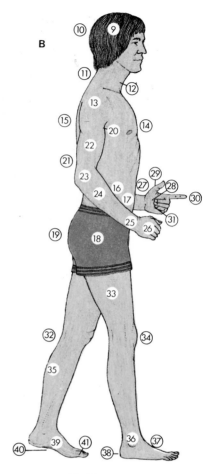

A. The skeleton
1 skull
2 collar-bone
3 shoulder-blade
4 breastbone
5 rib
6 backbone/spine
7 hip-bone/pelvis
8 kneecap

B. The body
9 hair
10 head
11 neck
12 throat
13 shoulder
14 chest
15 back
16 waist
17 stomach/tummy

18 hip
19 bottom/buttocks
20 armpit
21 arm
22 upper arm
23 elbow
24 forearm
25 wrist
26 fist
27 hand
28 palm
29 thumb
30 finger
31 nail
32 leg
33 thigh
34 knee
35 calf
36 ankle
37 foot

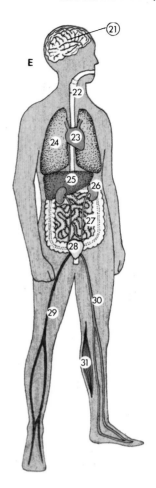

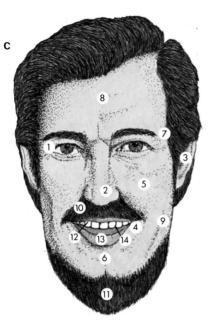

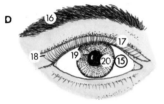

38 heel
39 instep
40 sole
41 toe

C. The face
1 eye
2 nose
3 ear
4 mouth
5 cheek
6 chin
7 temple
8 forehead/brow
9 jaw
10 moustache
11 beard
12 tooth
13 lip
14 tongue

D. The eye
15 eyeball
16 eyebrow
17 eyelid
18 eyelashes
19 pupil
20 iris

E. The insides
21 brain
22 windpipe
23 heart
24 lung
25 liver
26 kidney
27 intestines
28 bladder
29 vein
30 artery
31 muscle

1 vest	10 wellington(-boot)
2 pants	11 T-shirt
3 dressing-gown	12 shorts
4 pyjamas	13 cardigan
5 slipper	14 sock
6 jumper	15 plimsoll/gym-shoe/
7 jeans	tennis-shoe *trainers.*
8 jacket	16 cap
9 shoe	

1	shirt	13	hat
2	collar	14	coat
3	cuff	15	lapel
4	tie	16	pocket
5	waistcoat	17	trousers
6	suit	18	turn-up
7	sleeve	19	scarf
8	shoe	20	glove
9	shoelace	21	watch
10	sole	22	watch-strap
11	heel	23	glasses *spectacles*
12	raincoat/mackintosh/mac	24	umbrella

1 bra/brassière	11 necklace
2 slip/petticoat	12 nail-file
3 pants	13 (powder-)compact
4 tights	14 mascara
5 shawl	15 nail-varnish/-polish
6 nightdress	16 scent/perfume
7 slipper	17 eye-shadow
8 ring	18 face-cream
9 bracelet	19 lipstick
10 ear-ring	

1 blouse	9 coat
2 skirt	10 belt
3 sock	11 buckle
4 hat/bonnet	12 shoe
5 jersey/jumper/sweater/	13 scarf
pullover	14 handkerchief
6 trousers	15 brooch
7 sandal	16 (hand)bag
8 dress	17 umbrella

1 letter-box
2 (pedestrian) crossing
3 stall (in the market)
4 barrow
5 taxi
6 bicycle
7 traffic-light
8 signpost
9 kerb

10 gutter
11 drain
12 park
13 bridge
14 van
15 lorry
16 crossroads
17 motorbike / motorcycle
18 pram

19 (block of) flats
20 office-block
21 advertisement
22 shop
23 shop-window
24 lamp-post
25 parking-meter
26 bus
27 (bus-)conductor

28 bus-stop
29 pavement
30 litter-bin/-basket
31 (tele)phone-box/
   call-box
32 car-park
33 car
34 road/street

16 The Law

A. Detection
1 policeman
2 helmet
3 uniform
4 police-station
5 police-car
6 police-dog
7 truncheon
8 handcuffs
9 torch
10 magnifying-glass
11 fingerprints
12 footprints

B. Prison/Gaol/Jail
13 warder
14 prisoner
15 cell
16 bars

C. Law court
17 jury
18 witness-box
19 witness
20 defendant/accused
21 dock
22 judge
23 lawyer
24 gown/robe
25 wig

A. Fire brigade/Fire service
1 fireman
2 helmet
3 hose(pipe)
4 nozzle
5 hydrant
6 (fire-)extinguisher
7 fire-engine
8 ladder
9 bell
10 fire-escape
11 fire
12 smoke
13 flame

B. At the dentist
14 dental nurse
15 dentist's chair

16 dentist
17 drill
18 light

C. A hospital ward
19 (hospital) bed
20 patient
21 doctor
22 stethoscope
23 sling
24 X-ray
25 nurse
26 crutch
27 bandage
28 thermometer
29 (box of) pills
30 (bottle of) medicine
31 (medicine) spoon
32 stretcher

1 teacher	15 pencil
2 blackboard	16 set-square
3 easel	17 pen
4 chalk	18 exercise-book
5 duster	19 textbook
6 platform	20 slide-rule
7 desk	21 map
8 schoolgirl/pupil	22 timetable
9 satchel/schoolbag	23 calendar
10 ruler	24 poster
11 compasses	25 paintbrushes
12 protractor	26 palette
13 glue/gum	27 paints
14 rubber	

1 balance/scales	12 Bunsen burner
2 pan	13 tripod
3 weights	14 rubber tubing
4 meter	15 beaker
5 dial	16 flask
6 needle/pointer	17 crystals
7 bench	18 pipette
8 stool	19 magnet
9 microscope	20 pestle
10 lens	21 mortar
11 slide	22 test-tube

1 shop-window	14 deep-freeze/freezer
2 cashier	15 shelf
3 cash-register	16 tinned food
4 cash-desk	17 fruit
5 customer	18 vegetables
6 (carrier-)bag	19 bread
7 basket	20 biscuits
8 (shop-)assistant	21 cakes
9 cheese	22 counter
10 milk	23 receipt
11 eggs	24 (bank-)notes
12 sausages	25 coins
13 meat	

1	desk	12	letter basket
2	telephone	13	wastepaper-basket
3	adding-machine/	14	fan
	calculator	15	switchboard
4	blotter/blotting-pad	16	operator
5	diary	17	calendar
6	(hole-)punch	18	file
7	stapler	19	filing-cabinet
8	staple	20	carbon-paper
9	paper-clip	21	typewriter
10	(sheet of) paper	22	secretary/typist
11	envelope	23	notebook/notepad

1 clerk	12 writing-paper
2 scales	13 postcard
3 counter	14 envelope
4 letter-box/post-box/	15 flap
pillar-box	16 telegram/cable
5 postman	17 postal order
6 mailbag	18 seal
7 airletter	19 sealing-wax
8 postmark	20 parcel
9 stamp	21 string
10 (airmail-)letter	22 label
11 address	

1 crane	14 workman
2 bricklayer	15 sand
3 rafters	16 cement
4 tiles	17 trowel
5 ladder	18 hod
6 rung	19 mattock
7 scaffolding	20 excavator
8 bricks	21 cement-/concrete-
9 waste-pipe	mixer
10 foundations	22 dumper-/tipper-truck
11 plank	23 (pneumatic) drill
12 pick(-axe)	24 skip
13 shovel	

1 (work)bench	9 spade
2 file	10 (garden) fork
3 sandpaper	11 shears
4 chisel	12 trowel
5 (pen-)knife	13 spanner
6 wrench	14 pincers
7 screwdriver	15 chopper
8 vice	

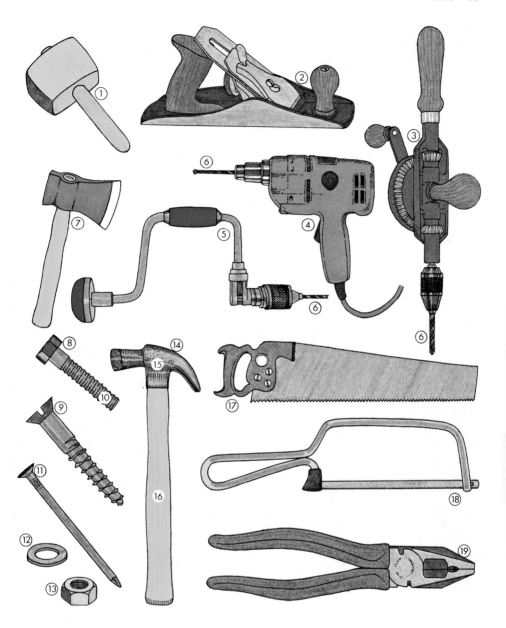

1 mallet
2 plane
3 hand-drill
4 electric drill
5 brace
6 bit
7 axe
8 bolt
9 screw
10 thread

11 nail
12 washer
13 nut
14 hammer
15 head
16 handle
17 saw
18 hacksaw
19 pliers

1 roof	12 shutter
2 chimney	13 window-box
3 wall	14 curtain
4 balcony	15 blind
5 patio	16 gutter
6 garage	17 drainpipe
7 (front) door	18 doormat
8 window	19 aerial
9 window-frame	20 (garden-)shed
10 window-pane	21 grass
11 (window-)ledge/sill	

The Weather

1 lightning
2 (storm-/thunder-) cloud
3 rain
4 raindrops
5 snow
6 snowball
7 snowman
8 icicle
9 sun
10 sky

In the Garden

11 tree
12 trunk
13 branch
14 twigs
15 leaves
16 gate
17 hedge
18 path
19 lawn
20 flower
21 flower-bed
22 shrub/bush
23 watering-can
24 flower-pot
25 (garden) fork
26 shed
27 wheelbarrow
28 washing line
29 washing
30 (clothes-) peg

1 door	16 stair
2 (door-)knocker	17 staircase
3 (door-)bell	18 banister
4 doorstep	19 handrail
5 letter-box	20 upstairs
6 keyhole	21 downstairs
7 lock and chain	22 light
8 bolt	23 (light-)switch
9 hinge	24 clock
10 (door)mat	25 telephone/phone
11 floor	26 receiver
12 rug	27 dial
13 (coat) rack	28 cord
14 peg	29 (tele)phone directory/
15 key	book

1 ceiling	22 radio
2 wall	23 (dining-)table
3 carpet	24 chair
4 fireplace	25 table-mat
5 mantelpiece	26 fork
6 fire	27 spoon
7 curtain	28 knife
8 armchair	29 glass
9 cushion	30 cup
10 bookcase	31 saucer
11 record-player	32 butter-dish
12 picture	33 coffee-pot
13 frame	34 spout
14 vase of flowers	35 lid
15 lamp	36 teapot
16 lampshade	37 (milk-)jug
17 television/TV	38 handle
18 (television) screen	39 (sugar-)bowl
19 coffee-table	40 bread-board
20 record	41 bread-knife
21 couch/settee/sofa	

1	cooker/stove	18	rolling-pin
2	oven	19	(cake-)tin
3	grill	20	jug
4	ring	21	tin-opener
5	refrigerator/fridge	22	tin/can
6	larder	23	basket
7	sink	24	cookery book
8	draining-board	25	colander
9	rubbish-bin	26	scourer
10	vegetable-rack	27	washing-up brush
11	frying-pan	28	washing-up liquid
12	pot/(sauce)pan	29	dish-cloth
13	kettle	30	sieve/strainer
14	tray	31	ladle
15	bread-bin	32	tea-towel/drying-up
16	shelf		cloth
17	(kitchen) scales		

1 vacuum-cleaner/
   hoover
2 broom
3 ironing-board
4 washing-machine
5 mop
6 brush
7 duster
8 dustpan
9 scouring powder

10 scrubbing-brush
11 iron
12 flex
13 (light-)bulb
14 hairdrier
15 plug
16 socket/power-point
17 switch
18 soap powder
19 bucket

The Bedroom
1 bed
2 headboard
3 pillow
4 pillow-case/-slip
5 sheet
6 blanket
7 bedspread
8 mattress
9 bedside table
10 dressing-table
11 stool
12 mirror
13 cupboard
14 wardrobe
15 chest-of-drawers
16 rug
17 clothes
18 clothes-brush
19 (coat-)hanger

20 (hair)brush
21 comb
22 box of tissues
23 jewellery box
24 (alarm-)clock
25 lamp

The Baby
26 cot
27 sleeping suit
28 dummy
29 teddy-bear
30 rattle
31 doll
32 potty
33 bottle
34 teat
35 bib
36 nappy

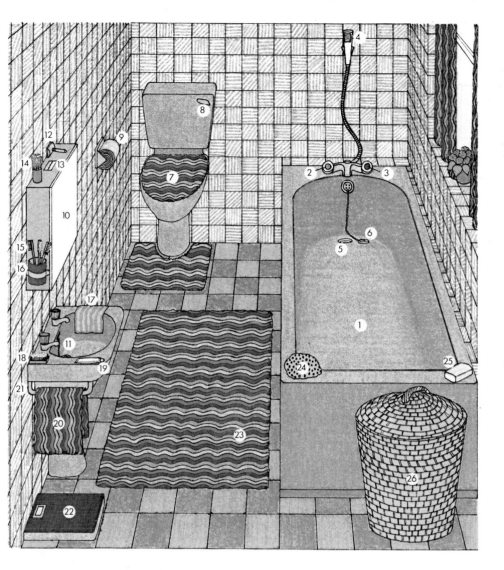

1 bath	14 shaving-brush
2 hot(-water) tap	15 toothbrush
3 cold(-water) tap	16 toothmug
4 shower	17 (face-)flannel
5 plug-hole	18 nailbrush
6 plug	19 (tube of) toothpaste
7 toilet/lavatory/loo	20 towel
8 handle	21 towel-rail
9 toilet-roll/toilet-paper/	22 (bathroom) scales.
lavatory-paper	23 bathmat
10 bathroom cabinet	24 sponge
11 (wash-)basin	25 soap
12 razor	26 laundry-basket
13 (razor) blade	

1 plateau	11 meadow
2 mountain	12 river
3 (mountain) peak	13 field
4 waterfall	14 hedge
5 lake	15 tree
6 valley	16 village
7 stream	17 (foot)path
8 wood	18 road
9 forest	19 pond
10 hill	

Camping
1 tent
2 groundsheet
3 sleeping-bag
4 rucksack
5 camping stove

At the Seaside
6 cliff
7 hotel
8 bungalow/chalet
9 promenade/sea-front
10 sea-wall
11 beach
12 sunshade
13 sunbather
14 (beach-)towel
15 mask/goggles
16 snorkel
17 ice-cream
18 windbreak

19 deckchair
20 swimming/bathing
   trunks
21 flipper
22 sand
23 sandcastle
24 bucket
25 spade
26 beachball
27 shell
28 pebbles
29 rocks
30 kite
31 sea
32 surf
33 wave
34 motor-boat
35 swimmer
36 swimming-/bathing-
   costume
37 seaweed

1 hayloft	19 plough
2 hay	20 furrow
3 cowshed	21 cow
4 barn	22 calf
5 pen	23 bull
6 farmyard	24 goats
7 farmhouse	25 beehive
8 field	26 shepherd
9 pond	27 crook
10 fence	28 sheepdog
11 fruit-tree	29 sheep
12 orchard	30 lamb
13 scarecrow	31 duckling
14 wheat	32 duck
15 farmer	33 hen/chicken
16 combine harvester	34 cock
17 irrigation canal	35 chick
18 tractor	

1 reservoir
2 dam
3 power-house
4 cable
5 pylon
6 power station
7 chimney

8 cooling tower
9 fuel
10 oil-derrick
11 oil-rig
12 pipeline
13 refinery
14 storage tank

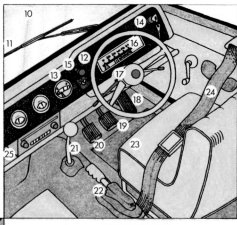

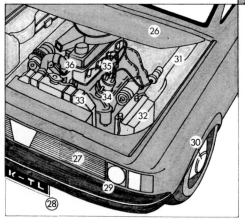

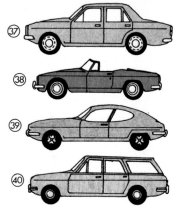

The (motor-)car

1 rear-mirror
2 boot
3 petrol-cap
4 rear light
5 indicator (light)
6 bumper
7 exhaust(-pipe)
8 tyre
9 aerial
10 windscreen
11 windscreen-wiper
12 dashboard
13 petrol gauge
14 ignition
15 choke
16 speedometer
17 steering-wheel
18 accelerator
19 (foot)brake
20 clutch

21 gear-lever
22 (hand)brake
23 seat
24 seat-/safety-belt
25 car radio
26 bonnet
27 radiator grill
28 number-plate
29 headlight
30 hubcap
31 engine
32 battery
33 radiator
34 distributor
35 sparking-plug
36 cylinder-head
37 saloon
38 convertible
39 coupé
40 estate

1 motorway	12 transporter
2 fly-over	13 caravan
3 underpass	14 lorry
4 roundabout	15 ambulance
5 outside lane	16 car
6 inside lane	17 coach
7 petrol-/service-station	18 sportscar
8 petrol-pump	19 tanker
9 air-pump	20 motorbike / motorcycle
10 attendant	21 trailer
11 articulated lorry	22 van

1 bicycle/bike/cycle	20 reflector
2 bell	21 horse
3 mirror	22 blinkers
4 cable	23 harness
5 headlamp	24 reins
6 handle-bars	25 whip
7 saddle	26 cart
8 saddlebag	27 crash-helmet
9 wheel	28 goggles
10 mudguard	29 scooter
11 tyre	30 rear light
12 spokes	31 seat
13 valve	32 accelerator/throttle
14 brake	33 brake
15 crossbar	34 pannier
16 pump	35 exhaust-pipe
17 pedal	36 starter
18 chain	37 footrest
19 cog	38 gear-lever

1 train	17 barrier
2 driver	18 waiting-room
3 engine	19 passengers
4 coach	20 platform
5 compartment	21 platform number
6 (ticket-)inspector	22 signalman
7 ticket	23 signal-box
8 seat	24 railway-line
9 luggage-rack	25 sleepers
10 guard	26 points
11 flag	27 signals
12 whistle	28 goods-truck/-waggon
13 station	29 buffer
14 ticket-office	30 siding
15 timetable	
16 ticket-collector	

1 horizon
2 pier
3 warehouse
4 crane
5 wharf/quay
6 cargo
7 ship
8 hold
9 funnel
10 gangway

11 anchor
12 dock
13 buoy
14 bollard
15 cable
16 windlass
17 fork-lift truck
18 hovercraft
19 tug

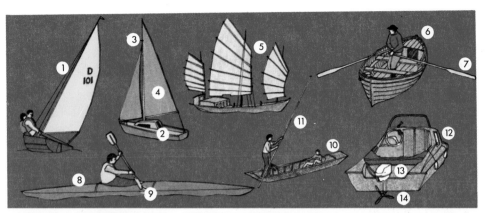

1 yacht	12 motor-boat/-launch
2 (cabin-)cruiser	13 outboard motor
3 mast	14 propeller
4 sail	15 ferry
5 junk	16 barge
6 rowing-boat	17 trawler
7 oar	18 (oil-)tanker
8 canoe	19 deck
9 paddle	20 liner
10 punt	21 funnel
11 pole	

1 customs hall	12 jet engine
2 customs officer	13 (tail-)fin
3 passport	14 glider
4 luggage/baggage	15 helicopter
5 captain	16 rotor
6 passenger	17 light aircraft
7 air-hostess	18 propeller
8 air-steward	19 runway
9 (aero)plane/airliner	20 control tower
10 fuselage	21 hangar
11 wing	

A. **Army**
1 soldier
2 rifle
3 bayonet
4 guided missile
5 jeep
6 gun
7 shell
8 tank
9 (hand-)grenade
10 pistol
11 bullet/cartridge
12 revolver
13 trigger
14 barrel
15 machine-gun

B. **Navy**
16 warship
17 torpedo
18 aircraft-carrier
19 submarine
20 periscope

C. **Air Force**
21 fighter plane
22 cockpit
23 bomber
24 bomb
25 parachute
26 navigator
27 pilot
28 control-panel

A. (Horse-)racing
1 jockey
2 (race-)horse
3 saddle
4 reins
5 bridle
6 bit
7 stirrup
8 riding breeches/
  jodhpurs
9 cap

B. Boxing
10 referee
11 boxer
12 glove
13 ring
14 ropes

C. Basketball
15 basket

16 backboard
17 ball

D. Hockey
18 stick

E. Table-tennis
19 bat
20 net
21 table

F. Wrestling
22 wrestlers

G. Judo
23 judo suit

H. Rugby
24 player
25 goal

A. Football/Soccer
1 (foot)ball
2 linesman
3 referee
4 whistle

B. Stadium
5 stand
6 pitch/field

C. Line-up
7 goal
8 goal-line
9 goal area
10 penalty area
11 penalty spot
12 touch line
13 halfway line
14 goalkeeper
15 left back ⎱ defenders
16 right back ⎰

17 left half ⎫ midfield
18 centre half ⎬ players
19 right half ⎭
20 outside left ⎫
21 inside left ⎪
22 centre forward ⎬ strikers
23 inside right ⎪
24 outside right ⎭

D. Winter Sports
25 skier
26 ski
27 (ski-)stick/pole
28 tobogganist
29 toboggan
30 skater
31 skate

A. Baseball
1 catcher
2 mask
3 glove
4 bat
5 batter

B. Cricket
6 batsman
7 bat
8 bails
9 wicket/stumps
10 cricket ball
11 wicket-keeper
12 pad
13 pitch
14 bowler
15 fielder

16 umpire
17 crease

C. Fishing
18 fisherman
19 rod
20 line
21 hook
22 bait

D. Tennis
23 (tennis-)court
24 net
25 server
26 service line
27 racket
28 tennis-ball

Orchestra

1 flute
2 clarinet
3 musician/player
4 violin
5 strings
6 bow
7 viola
8 cello
9 double-bass
10 conductor
11 baton
12 (sheet) music
13 rostrum
14 horn
15 piano
16 keys

17 pedal
18 stool
19 trumpet
20 trombone
21 slide
22 saxophone
23 mouthpiece

Pop Group

24 singer
25 microphone/mike
26 (electric) guitar
27 amplifier
28 loudspeaker
29 cymbals
30 drum

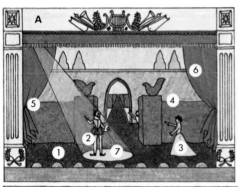

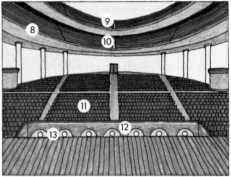

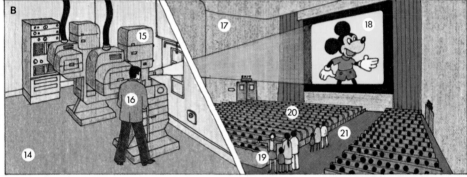

A. The Theatre
1 stage
2 actor
3 actress
4 set
5 wings
6 curtain
7 spotlight
8 theatre
9 gallery
10 circle/balcony
11 stalls
12 (orchestra) pit
13 footlights

B. The Cinema
14 projection room
15 projector
16 projectionist
17 cinema
18 screen
19 usherette
20 seats
21 aisle/gangway

C. The Library
22 librarian
23 card-index
24 counter/desk
25 bookshelf

1 (beer-)bottle
2 bottle-top
3 beer-mug
4 (beer-)can
5 matchbox
6 match
7 bottle-opener
8 cigarette
9 ash
10 ashtray
11 corkscrew
12 straw
13 soft drink
14 tankard
15 juke-box
16 bar

17 barmaid
18 barman
19 pump
20 (bar-)stool
21 waiter
22 customer
23 menu
24 bottle of wine
25 cork
26 (wine-)glass
27 salt(-cellar)
28 mustard(-pot)
29 pepper(-pot)
30 table-cloth
31 napkin/serviette

A

B

C

D

A. Chess and Draughts
1 (set of) chessmen/
  chess pieces
2 board
3 pawn
4 rook/castle
5 knight
6 bishop
7 queen
8 king
9 draughts

B. Cards
10 (pack of)
  (playing-)cards
11 jack/knave of clubs
12 queen of diamonds
13 king of hearts
14 ace of spades

C. Reading
15 book
16 cover
17 (dust-)jacket
18 spine
19 page
20 illustration
21 text

D. Photography
22 print/photograph
  photo/snapshot
23 negative
24 (roll of) film
25 camera
26 lens
27 screen
28 stand
29 (slide-)projector
30 slide

1 sewing-machine	15 button
2 tape	16 button-hole
3 seam	17 stitch
4 hem	18 knitting-needle
5 thimble	19 wool
6 needle	20 pattern
7 elastic	21 knitting
8 reel of cotton	22 zip/zipper/zip-fastener
9 lace	23 hook and eye
10 safety-pin	24 ribbon
11 pleat	25 tape-measure
12 pin	26 scissors
13 material/cloth	27 press-stud
14 frill	

1 hairdresser	9 typist
2 butcher	10 dressmaker
3 carpenter	11 waitress
4 bank-clerk	12 driver
5 mechanic	13 clown
6 docker	14 porter
7 miner	15 announcer
8 artist	

1 greengrocer
2 electrician
3 gardener
4 photographer
5 florist
6 barber
7 baker
8 doctor

9 salesman
10 nurse
11 teacher
12 soldier
13 policeman
14 optician
15 sailor

1 horse	14 puppy
2 foal	15 cat
3 pig	16 kitten
4 snout	17 paw
5 llama	18 mouse
6 camel	19 squirrel
7 hump	20 rabbit
8 buffalo	21 whisker
9 horn	22 rat
10 donkey	23 tail
11 reindeer	24 fox
12 antler	25 bat
13 dog	26 hedgehog

1 whale	14 gorilla
2 fluke	15 giraffe
3 dolphin	16 lion
4 fin	17 mane
5 antelope	18 leopard
6 kangaroo	19 tiger
7 pouch	20 hippopotamus
8 bear	21 elephant
9 seal	22 trunk
10 flipper	23 tusk
11 wolf	24 zebra
12 baboon	25 rhinoceros
13 monkey	26 horn

Fish and other animals

1 shark
2 fin
3 swordfish
4 salmon
5 gill
6 herring
7 tail
8 mouth
9 scales
10 eel
11 jelly-fish
12 lobster
13 snail

14 shell
15 sunfish
16 oyster
17 crab
18 pincer/claw
19 slug
20 frog
21 worm
22 centipede
23 octopus
24 tentacle
25 spider
26 (cob)web
27 scorpion

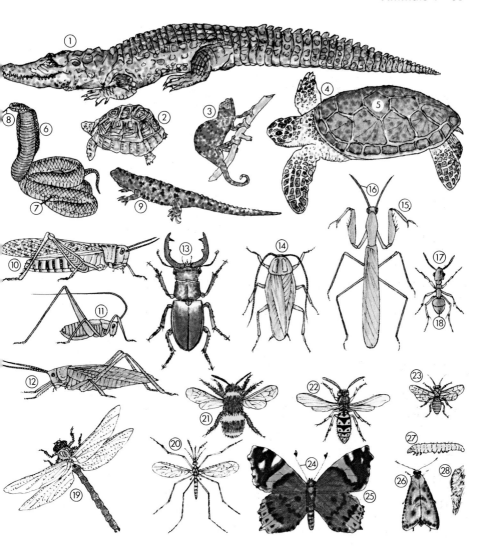

Reptiles
1 crocodile
2 tortoise
3 chameleon
4 turtle
5 shell
6 snake
7 coil
8 tongue
9 lizard

Insects
10 locust
11 cricket
12 grasshopper
13 beetle

14 cockroach
15 mantis
16 feeler
17 ant
18 abdomen
19 dragonfly
20 mosquito
21 bee
22 wasp
23 fly
24 antenna
25 butterfly
26 moth
27 caterpillar
28 cocoon

Birds

1 ostrich
2 eagle
3 claw
4 beak
5 feathers
6 hawk
7 owl
8 flamingo
9 webbed foot
10 vulture
11 peacock
12 crest
13 penguin
14 pheasant
15 heron
16 turkey
17 swan

18 canary
19 bill
20 parrot
21 (sea)gull
22 swallow
23 wing
24 dove
25 goose
26 budgerigar
27 humming-bird
28 sparrow
29 nest
30 kingfisher
31 pigeon
32 blackbird
33 crow

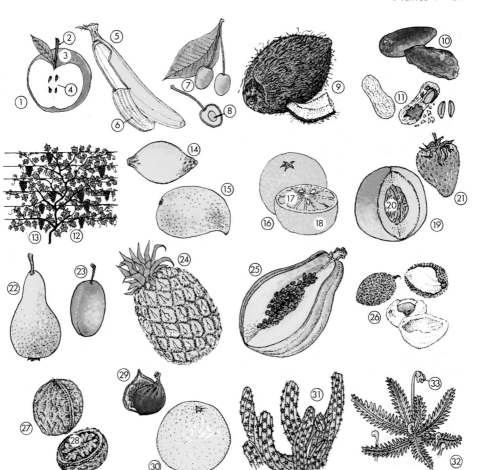

Fruit	18 peel/rind
1 apple	19 peach
2 stalk	20 stone
3 peel	21 strawberry
4 core	22 pear
5 banana	23 plum
6 skin	24 pineapple
7 cherry	25 pawpaw/papaya
8 stone	26 lychee
9 coconut	27 walnut
10 date	28 kernel
11 peanut/groundnut	29 fig
12 grapes	30 grapefruit
13 vine	31 cactus
14 lemon	32 fern
15 mango	33 frond
16 orange	
17 segments	

Vegetables

1 bean
2 stalk
3 pea
4 pod
5 carrot
6 potato
7 marrow
8 cucumber
9 beetroot
10 cauliflower
11 cabbage
12 lettuce
13 onion
14 mushroom
15 tomato
16 aubergine/eggplant

Flowers

17 daffodil
18 daisy
19 rose
20 petal
21 orchid
22 tulip
23 stem
24 hibiscus
25 bud
26 waterlily
27 sunflower
28 seeds

1 corn/maize	13 branch/bough
2 ear of wheat	14 twig
3 olive	15 leaf
4 cocoa pod	16 acorn
5 coffee berry	17 bark
6 cotton	18 log
7 rice	19 palm
8 tea	20 fir
9 sugar-cane	21 cone
10 oak tree	22 needles
11 roots	23 cedar
12 trunk	24 willow

1 blow	14 dream
2 break	15 drive
3 carry	16 drown
4 catch	17 eat
5 climb	18 fall
6 crawl	19 fight
7 cry/weep	20 fly
8 cut	21 jump/leap
9 dance	22 kick
10 dig	23 kneel
11 dive	24 laugh
12 draw	25 lick
13 drink	

1 listen	14 sing
2 open	15 sit
3 lie	16 smile
4 paint	17 stand
5 pull	18 stir
6 push	19 sweep
7 read	20 swim
8 ride	21 tear
9 run	22 touch
10 sail	23 tie
11 sew	24 walk
12 shoot	25 wash
13 shut	

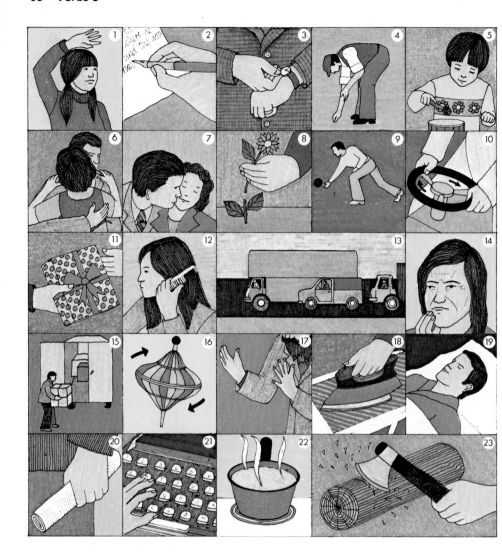

1 wave	13 pass/overtake
2 write	14 frown
3 wind	15 put
4 bend	16 spin
5 hit/beat	17 clap
6 hug	18 iron
7 kiss	19 sleep
8 pick	20 hold
9 throw	21 type
10 turn	22 boil
11 give	23 chop
12 comb	

1 carton
2 urn
3 briefcase
4 barrel
5 (hand)bag
6 purse
7 paper-bag
8 dustbin
9 thermos/vacuum-flask
10 (shopping) basket

11 crate
12 trunk
13 sack
14 cage
15 carrier-bag
16 wallet
17 (suit)case
18 holdall
19 box
20 safe
21 (water-)tank

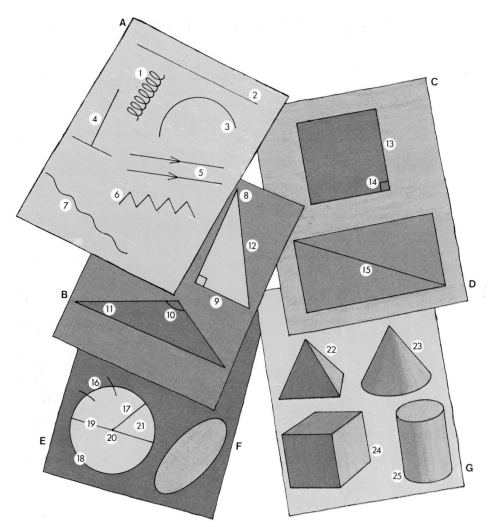

A. Lines
1 spiral
2 straight line
3 curve
4 perpendicular line
5 parallel lines
6 zig-zag
7 wavy line

B. Triangles
8 apex
9 base
10 obtuse angle
11 acute angle
12 hypotenuse

C. Square
13 side
14 right angle

D. Rectangle/Oblong
15 diagonal

E. Circle
16 arc
17 radius
18 circumference
19 diameter
20 centre
21 sector

F. Oval/Ellipse

G. Solid Figures
22 pyramid
23 cone
24 cube
25 cylinder

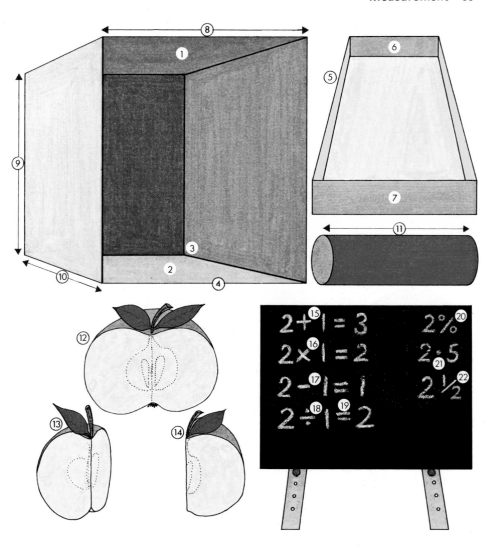

1 top
2 bottom
3 corner
4 edge
5 side
6 back
7 front
8 width
9 height
10 depth
11 length

12 a half
13 a third
14 a quarter
15 plus
16 multiplied by
17 minus
18 divided by
19 equals
20 per cent
21 decimal point
22 fraction

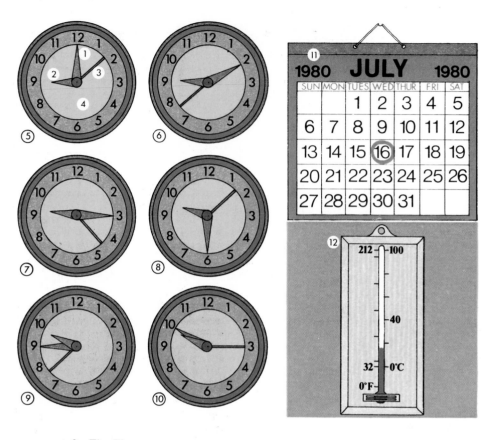

A. **The Time**
1 minute-hand
2 hour-hand
3 second-hand
4 clock-face
5 nine o'clock: 9.00
6 ten past nine/nine ten: 9.10
7 (a) quarter past nine/nine fifteen: 9.15
8 half past nine/nine thirty: 9.30
9 a quarter to ten/nine forty-five: 9.45
10 ten to ten/nine fifty: 9.50

B. **The Date**
11 calendar
Today's date is Wednesday the sixteenth of July, nineteen eighty:
16th July 1980 or 16/7/80.

C. **The Temperature**
12 thermometer
The temperature is 18 degrees centigrade (18°C) or 65 degrees
Fahrenheit (65°F).

1 Alan and Ann are **husband** and **wife**.
2 Their **children** are Betty and Bob.
3 Their **daughter** is Betty and their **son** is Bob.
4 Alan is Bob's **father** and Ann is Bob's **mother**.
5 Betty is Bob's **sister** and Bob is Betty's **brother**.
6 Alan is Ben's **father-in-law** and Ann is his **mother-in-law**.
7 Ben is Alan and Ann's **son-in-law** and Brenda is their **daughter-in-law**.
8 Ben is Bob's **brother-in-law** and Brenda is Betty's **sister-in-law**
9 Colin is Cliff and Carol's **cousin**.
10 Betty is Colin's **aunt** and Ben is his **uncle**.
11 Colin is Betty's **nephew** and Carol is Bob's **niece**.
12 Cliff is Ann and Alan's **grandson** and Carol is their **granddaughter**.

1 bunch (of flowers)	9 heap (of stones)
2 bundle (of sticks)	10 herd (of cows)
3 crowd (of people)	11 party (of tourists)
4 fleet (of ships)	12 pile (of blankets)
5 flight (of stairs)	13 plate (of sandwiches)
6 flock (of sheep or birds)	14 row (of houses)
7 gang (of workmen)	15 team (of players)
8 string (of beads)	16 swarm (of bees)

1 ball (of string, wool)
2 bar (of chocolate)
3 tablet/bar (of soap)
4 joint (of meat)
5 line (of washing)
6 loaf (of bread)
7 lump (of sugar)
8 slice/piece (of cake)

9   reel (of cotton)
10 box (of matches)/
    packet (of cigarettes)
11 packet (of tea)
12 roll (of paper)
13 tube (of toothpaste)
14 bowl (of soup)

1 a) big/large	9 a) fast
b) little/small	b) slow
2 a) blunt	10 a) fat
b) sharp	b) thin
3 a) clean	11 a) happy
b) dirty	b) sad
4 a) closed/shut	12 a) easy
b) open	b) difficult/hard
5 a) crooked	13 a) soft
b) straight	b) hard
6 a) shallow	14 a) high
b) deep	b) low
7 a) wet	15 a) hot
b) dry	b) cold
8 a) empty	16 a) long
b) full	b) short

1 a) narrow b) wide	9 a) pretty/beautiful b) ugly
2 a) young b) old	10 a) first b) last
3 a) new b) old	11 a) light b) dark
4 a) calm b) rough	12 a) light b) heavy
5 a) rough b) smooth	13 a) loud b) soft
6 a) strong b) weak	14 a) solid b) hollow
7 a) tidy b) untidy	15 a) thick b) thin
8 a) good b) bad	16 a) loose b) tight

1 **outside** the room
2 **through** the door
3 **below** the picture
4 **down** the wall
5 **up** the wall
6 **round** the neck
7 **in front of** the chair
8 **against** the wall
9 **into** the drawer
10 **in/inside** the drawer

11 **out of** the drawer
12 **on** the table
13 **on to/onto** the table
14 **beside/next to** the table
15 **by/near** the chair
16 **behind** the chair
17 **under/underneath** the table

1 **above** the trees
2 **beyond** the bridge
3 **from** the sea
4 **to** the sea
5 **among** the trees
6 **off** the road
7 **across/over** the road

8 **at** the corner
9 **along** the road
10 **towards** the bridge
11 **away from** the bridge
12 **between** the cars

A. **This** boy is Paul. **He** is holding **his** football. **It** is **his**. He says, "**I** am Paul. **This** is **my** football. It is **mine. Its** colours are black and white."

B. This girl is Mary. **She** is riding **her** bicycle. It is **hers**. She says, "My father gave it to **me**."

C. Paul and Mary have a dog. He is **theirs. They** are feeding **their** dog. Bob is watching **them.** Mary says to Bob, "This is **our** dog. He is **ours.** He belongs to **us. We** are feeding **him**." Bob says, "This is water for **your** dog."

D. Paul says to Bob, "**Who** is **that** girl **there?**" Bob says, "**That** is Julie. She is coming **here**."

E. Bob says to Julie, "**What** are **those** things **you** are carrying?" Julie says, "**These** are oranges." Paul says, "**Whose** oranges are they?" Julie says, "They are for **you** and Bob. They are **yours**." Bob says, "**Which** one is mine?" Julie says, "This one here. But **where** is Mary? **This** one is for **her**."

Colours

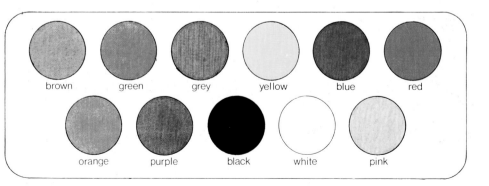

brown   green   grey   yellow   blue   red

orange   purple   black   white   pink

0	nought, zero, nothing	40	forty
1	one	50	fifty
2	two	60	sixty
3	three	70	seventy
4	four	80	eighty
5	five	90	ninety
6	six	100	a/one hundred
7	seven	500	five hundred
8	eight	621	six hundred and
9	nine		twenty-one
10	ten		
11	eleven	1,000	a/one thousand
12	twelve	1,000,000	a million
13	thirteen		
14	fourteen	1st	first
15	fifteen	2nd	second
16	sixteen	3rd	third
17	seventeen	4th	fourth
18	eighteen	5th	fifth
19	nineteen	6th	sixth
20	twenty	7th	seventh
21	twenty-one	8th	eighth
30	thirty	9th	ninth
		10th	tenth
		20th	twentieth

Weight
1,000 grams (gm) = 1 kilogram (kg)

Length
10 millimetres (mm) = 1 centimetre (cm)
100 centimetres = 1 metre (m)
1,000 metres = 1 kilometre (km)

Liquids
1,000 millilitres (ml) = 1 litre (l)

Time
60 seconds = 1 minute (min)
60 minutes = 1 hour (hr)
24 hours = 1 day
7 days = 1 week (wk)
365 days = 1 year (yr)
12 months = 1 year
100 years = 1 century (c)

Days of the Week
Monday, Tuesday, Wednesday, Thursday, Friday, Saturday, Sunday.

Months of the Year
January, February, March, April, May, June, July, August, September, October, November, December.

Vowels and diphthongs

iː	as in *sea*	/siː/	ʊ	as in *book*	/bʊk/	aɪ	as in *five*	/faɪv/
ɪ	as in *sit*	/sɪt/	uː	as in *root*	/ruːt/	aʊ	as in *mouse*	/maʊs/
e	as in *ten*	/ten/	ʌ	as in *cup*	/kʌp/	ɔɪ	as in *toy*	/tɔɪ/
æ	as in *hat*	/hæt/	ɜː	as in *fur*	/fɜː(r)/	ɪə	as in *near*	/nɪə(r)/
ɑː	as in *farm*	/fɑːm/	ə	as in *away*	/ə'weɪ/	eə	as in *hair*	/heə(r)/
ɒ	as in *pot*	/pɒt/	eɪ	as in *page*	/peɪdʒ/	ʊə	as in *pure*	/pjʊə(r)/
ɔː	as in *ball*	/bɔːl/	əʊ	as in *hole*	/həʊl/			

Consonants

p	as in *pen*	/pen/	f	as in *five*	/faɪv/	h	as in *hair*	/heə(r)/
b	as in *ball*	/bɔːl/	v	as in *van*	/væn/	m	as in *mouse*	/maʊs/
t	as in *toy*	/tɔɪ/	θ	as in *thin*	/θɪn/	n	as in *neck*	/nek/
d	as in *dog*	/dɒg/	ð	as in *there*	/ðeə(r)/	ŋ	as in *wing*	/wɪŋ/
k	as in *cat*	/kæt/	s	as in *sea*	/siː/	l	as in *ball*	/bɔːl/
g	as in *goat*	/gəʊt/	z	as in *zip*	/zɪp/	r	as in *root*	/ruːt/
tʃ	as in *chin*	/tʃɪn/	ʃ	as in *she*	/ʃiː/	j	as in *year*	/jɜː(r)/
dʒ	as in *jaw*	/dʒɔː/	ʒ	as in *measure*	/'meʒə(r)/	w	as in *wing*	/wɪŋ/

/'/ is a *principal* (primary or strong) stress as in *pineapple* /'paɪnæpl/.
/ˌ/ is a *subordinate* (secondary/weak) stress as in *magazine* /ˌmægə'ziːn/.
(r) means that /r/ is pronounced only when the following word begins with a vowel, as in
fire /'faɪə(r)/, *fire-engine* /'faɪər endʒɪn/.

Nouns are usually entered here in their *singular* form. The majority form their plural
regularly, by adding 's' or 'es' if they end in 's', 'ss', 'ch', 'x', 'sh', or by adding 'ies'
in place of a 'y'. There are some which have irregular plural forms (foot/feet, man/
men, potato/potatoes, scarf/scarves, etc.) If you are in doubt about the plural form
of a noun listed in the index, look it up in your dictionary or grammar book. Those
nouns which are (usually) used in the *singular* only are marked ‡. Nouns which are
(usually) used in the *plural* only are marked †. Some nouns have an identical form
for singular and plural use; these are marked ‡†.

Index

abdomen /'æbdəmən/ 59/18
above /ə'bʌv/ 77/1
accelerator /ək'seləreɪtə(r)/ 38/18; 40/32
accused /ə'kjuːzd/ 16/20
ace /eɪs/ 52/14
acorn /'eɪkɔːn/ 63/16
across /ə'krɒs/ 77/7
actor /'æktə(r)/ 50/2
actress /'æktrɪs/ 50/3
acute /ə'kjuːt/ 68/11
adding-machine /'ædɪŋ məʃiːn/ 21/3
address /ə'dres/ 22/11
adjective /'ædʒɪktɪv/ 74–75
adverb /'ædvɜːb/ 78
advertisement /əd'vɜːtɪsmənt/ 15/21
aerial /'eərɪəl/ 26/19; 38/9
aeroplane /'eərəpleɪn/ 44/9
Africa /'æfrɪkə/ 6/4
against /ə'genst/ 76/8
air /eə(r)/ 44
‡†aircraft /'eəkrɑːft/ 44/17
-'aircraft-carrier 45/18
air force /'eə fɔːs/ 45/C
'air-hostess 44/7
'airletter 22/7
'airliner 44/9
'airmail 22/10
‡'airport 44
'air-pump 39/9
'air-steward 44/8
aisle /aɪl/ 50/21
alarm-clock /ə'lɑːm klɒk/ 32/24
Alaska /ə'læskə/ 6/15
along /ə'lɒŋ/ 77/9
Alps /ælps/ 7/38
Amazon /'æməzən/ 7/46
ambulance /'æmbjʊləns/ 39/15
America /ə'merɪkə/ 6/1, 2
among /ə'mʌŋ/ 77/5
amplifier /'æmplɪfaɪə(r)/ 49/27

anchor /'æŋkə(r)/ 42/11
Andes /'ændiːz/ 7/37
angle /'æŋgl/ 68/10, 11, 14
animal /'ænɪml/ 56–60
ankle /'æŋkl/ 8/36
announcer /ə'naʊnsə(r)/ 54/15
ant /ænt/ 59/17
Antarctic /ænt'ɑːktɪk/ 5/6; 6/14
Antarctica /ænt'ɑːktɪkə/ 6/7
antelope /'æntɪləʊp/ 57/5
antenna /æn'tenə/ 59/24
antler /'æntlə(r)/ 56/12
apex /'eɪpeks/ 68/8
apple /'æpl/ 61/1
April /'eɪprəl/ 80
Arabian Desert /ə,reɪbɪən 'dezət/ 7/43
Arabian Sea /ə,reɪbɪən 'siː/ 6/27
arc /ɑːk/ 68/16
Arctic /'ɑːktɪk/ 5/2; 6/8
area /'eərɪə/ 47/9, 10
arm /ɑːm/ 8/21, 22
ˌarm'chair 29/8
armpit 8/20
Army /'ɑːmi/ 45/A
artery /'ɑːtəri/ 9/30
articulated lorry /ɑː,tɪkjʊleɪtɪd 'lɒri/ 39/11
artist /'ɑːtɪst/ 54/8
ash /æʃ/ 51/9
ashtray /'æʃtreɪ/ 51/10
Asia /'eɪʃə/ 6/5
assistant /ə'sɪstənt/ 20/8
astronaut /'æstrənɔːt/ 4/20
at /æt/ 77/8
Atlantic /ət'læntɪk/ 6/11, 12
attendant /ə'tendənt/ 39/10
aubergine /'əʊbəʒiːn/ 62/16
August /'ɔːgəst/ 80
aunt /ɑːnt/ 71/10
Australia /ɒ'streɪlɪə/ 6/6
away /ə'weɪ/ 77/11
axe /æks/ 23/12; 25/7

baboon /bə'buːn/ 57/12
baby /'beɪbi/ 32/B
back /bæk/ 8/15; 47/15, 16; 69/6
backboard /'bækbɔːd/ 46/16
backbone /'bækbəʊn/ 8/6
bad /bæd/ 75/8
bag /bæg/ 13/16; 20/6; 35/3; 67/5, 7, 15
†baggage /'bægɪdʒ/ 44/4
bail /beɪl/ 48/8
‡†bait /beɪt/ 48/22
baker /'beɪkə(r)/ 55/7
balance /'bæləns/ 19/1
balcony /'bælkəni/ 26/4; 50/10
ball /bɔːl/ 35/26; 46/17; 47/1; 48/10, 28; 73/1
Baltic Sea /ˌbɔːltɪk 'siː/ 6/21
banana /bə'nɑːnə/ 61/5
bandage /'bændɪdʒ/ 17/27
banister /'bænɪstə(r)/ 28/18
bank-clerk /'bæŋk klɑːk/ 54/4
banknote /'bæŋknəʊt/ 20/24
bar /bɑː(r)/ 16/16; 51; 73/2, 3
barber /'bɑːbə(r)/ 55/6
barge /bɑːdʒ/ 43/16
bark /bɑːk/ 63/17
barmaid /'bɑːmeɪd/ 51/17
barman /'bɑːmən/ 51/18
barn /bɑːn/ 36/4
barrel /'bærəl/ 45/14; 67/4
barrier /'bærɪə(r)/ 41/17
barrow /'bærəʊ/ 14/4
'bar-stool 51/20
base /beɪs/ 68/9
‡baseball /'beɪsbɔːl/ 48/A
basin /'beɪsn/ 33/11
basket /'bɑːskɪt/ 15/30; 20/7; 21/12, 13;
30/23; 33/26; 46/15; 67/10
‡basketball /'bɑːskɪtbɔːl/ 46/C
bass /beɪs/ 49/9
bat /bæt/ 46/19; 48/4, 7; 56/25
bath /bɑːθ/ 33/1
bathing-costume /'beɪðɪŋ kɒstjuːm/ 35/36

†bathing trunks /'beɪðɪŋ trʌŋks/ 35/20
bathmat /'bɑːθmæt/ 33/23
bathroom /'bɑːθrʊm/ 33
baton /'bætən/ 49/11
batsman /'bætsmən/ 48/6
batter /'bætə(r)/ 48/5
battery /'bætərɪ/ 38/32
bay /beɪ/ 5/8; 6/C
bayonet /'beɪənɪt/ 45/3
beach /biːtʃ/ 35/11
beachball 35/26
beak /biːk/ 60/4
beaker /'biːkə(r)/ 19/15
bean /biːn/ 62/1
bear /beə(r)/ 57/8
beard /bɪəd/ 9/11
beat /biːt/ 66/5
beautiful /'bjuːtəfl/ 75/9
bed /bed/ 17/19; 27/21; 32/1
bedroom /'bedrʊm/ 32
bedside table /'bedsaɪd 'teɪbl/ 32/9
bedspread /'bedspred/ 32/7
bee /biː/ 59/21
beehive /'biːhaɪv/ 36/25
beer /bɪə(r)/ 51/1
beetle /'biːtl/ 59/13
beetroot /'biːtruːt/ 62/9
behind /bɪ'haɪnd/ 76/16
bell /bel/ 17/9; 28/3; 40/2
below /bɪ'ləʊ/ 76/3
belt /belt/ 13/10; 38/24
bench /bentʃ/ 19/7; 24/1
bend /bend/ 66/4
Bengal (Bay of) /,beŋ'gɔːl/ 6/28
Bering Sea /,beərɪŋ 'siː/ 7/35
berry /'berɪ/ 63/5
beside /bɪ'saɪd/ 76/14
between /bɪ'twiːn/ 77/12
beyond /bɪ'jɒnd/ 77/2
bib /bɪb/ 32/35
bicycle /'baɪsɪkl/ 14/6; 40/1
big /bɪg/ 74/1
bike /baɪk/ 40/1
bill /bɪl/ 60/19
bin /bɪn/ 15/30; 30/9, 15
bird /bɜːd/ 60
biscuit /'bɪskɪt/ 20/20
bishop /'bɪʃəp/ 52/6
bit /bɪt/ 25/6; 46/6
black /blæk/ 79
blackbird /'blækbɜːd/ 60/32
blackboard /'blækbɔːd/ 18/2
Black Sea /,blæk 'siː/ 6/23
bladder /'blædə(r)/ 9/28
blade /bleɪd/ 33/13
blanket /'blæŋkɪt/ 32/6
blind /blaɪnd/ 26/15
blinkers /'blɪŋkəz/ 40/22
block /blɒk/ 15/19, 20
blotter /'blɒtə(r)/ 21/4
blotting-pad /'blɒtɪŋ pæd/ 21/4
blouse /blaʊz/ 13/1
blow /bləʊ/ 64/1
blue /bluː/ 79
blunt /blʌnt/ 74/2
board /bɔːd/ 29/40; 52/2
boat /bəʊt/ 35/34; 43/6, 12
body /'bɒdɪ/ 8–9
boil /bɔɪl/ 66/22
bollard /'bɒləd/ 42/14
bolt /bəʊlt/ 25/8; 28/8
bomb /bɒm/ 45/24
bomber /'bɒmə(r)/ 45/23
bone /bəʊn/ 8/A
bonnet /'bɒnɪt/ 13/43; 38/26
book /bʊk/ 18/18, 19; 28/29; 30/24; 52/15
bookcase /'bʊkkeɪs/ 29/10
bookshelf /'bʊkʃelf/ 50/25
boot /buːt/ 10/10; 38/2
bottle /'bɒtl/ 17/30; 33/33; 51/1, 24
bottom /'bɒtəm/ 8/19; 69/2
bough /baʊ/ 63/13
bowl /bəʊl/ 29/39; 73/14
bowler /'bəʊlə(r)/ 48/14
box /bɒks/ 14/1; 15/31; 16/18; 17/29; 22/4;
  26/13; 28/5; 32/22, 23; 51/15; 67/19; 73/10
boxer /'bɒksə(r)/ 46/11
‡boxing /'bɒksɪŋ/ 46/B
boy /bɔɪ/ 10
bra /brɑː/ 12/1
brace /breɪs/ 25/5
bracelet /'breɪslɪt/ 12/9
brain /breɪn/ 9/21

brake /breɪk/ 38/19, 22; 40/14, 33
branch /brɑːntʃ/ 27/13; 63/13
brassière /'bræsɪə(r)/ 12/1
‡bread /bred/ 20/19
break /breɪk/ 64/2
breastbone /'brestbəʊn/ 8/4
†breeches /'brɪtʃɪz/ 46/18
brick /brɪk/ 23/8
bricklayer /'brɪkleɪə(r)/ 23/2
bridge /brɪdʒ/ 14/13
bridle /'braɪdl/ 46/5
briefcase /'briːfkeɪs/ 67/3
brigade /brɪ'geɪd/ 17/A
brooch /brəʊtʃ/ 13/15
broom /bruːm/ 31/2
brother /'brʌðə(r)/ 71/5
brother-in-law /'brʌðər ɪn lɔː/ 71/8
brow /braʊ/ 9/8
brown /braʊn/ 79
brush /brʌʃ/ 30/27; 31/6, 10; 32/18, 20;
  33/14, 15, 18
bucket /'bʌkɪt/ 31/19; 35/24
buckle /'bʌkl/ 13/11
bud /bʌd/ 62/25
budgerigar /'bʌdʒərɪgɑː(r)/ 60/26
buffalo /'bʌfələʊ/ 56/8
buffer /'bʌfə(r)/ 41/29
building /'bɪldɪŋ/ 23
bulb /bʌlb/ 31/13
bull /bʊl/ 36/23
bullet /'bʊlɪt/ 45/11
bumper /'bʌmpə(r)/ 38/6
bunch /bʌntʃ/ 72/1
bundle /'bʌndl/ 72/2
bungalow /'bʌŋgələʊ/ 35/8
Bunsen burner /,bʌnsən 'bɜːnə(r)/ 19/12
buoy /bɔɪ/ 42/13
bus /bʌs/ 15/26
bush /bʊʃ/ 27/22
'bus-stop 15/28
butcher /'bʊtʃə(r)/ 54/2
butter-dish /'bʌtə dɪʃ/ 29/32
butterfly /'bʌtəflaɪ/ 59/25
buttocks /'bʌtəks/ 8/19
button /'bʌtn/ 53/15
'button-hole 53/16
by /baɪ/ 76/15

cabbage /'kæbɪdʒ/ 62/11
cabin-cruiser /'kæbɪn kruːzə(r)/ 43/2
cabinet /'kæbɪnɪt/ 29/19; 33/10
cable /'keɪbl/ 22/16; 37/4; 40/4; 42/15
cactus /'kæktəs/ 61/31
cage /keɪdʒ/ 67/14
cake /keɪk/ 20/21
'cake-tin 30/19
calculator /'kælkjʊleɪtə(r)/ 21/3
calendar /'kælɪndə(r)/ 18/23; 21/17; 70/11
calf /kɑːf/ 8/35; 36/22
call-box /'kɔːl bɒks/ 15/31
calm /kɑːm/ 75/4
camel /'kæml/ 56/6
camera /'kæmərə/ 52/25
‡camping /'kæmpɪŋ/ 35/A
can /kæn/ 27/23; 30/22; 51/4
canal /kə'næl/ 36/17
canary /kə'neərɪ/ 60/18
Cancer /'kænsə(r)/ 5/3
cane /keɪn/ 63/9
canoe /kə'nuː/ 43/8
cap /kæp/ 10/16; 38/3; 46/9
Capricorn /'kæprɪkɔːn/ 5/5
capsule /'kæpsjuːl/ 4/19
captain /'kæptɪn/ 44/5
car /kɑː/ 13/33; 16/5; 38; 39/16
caravan /'kærəvæn/ 39/13
‡carbon-paper /'kɑːbən peɪpə(r)/ 21/20
card /kɑːd/ 52/B
card-index /'kɑːd ɪndeks/ 50/23
cardigan /'kɑːdɪgən/ 10/13
cargo /'kɑːgəʊ/ 42/6
Caribbean /,kærɪ'biːən/ 6/18
'car-park 15/32
carpenter /'kɑːpəntə(r)/ 54/3
carpet /'kɑːpɪt/ 29/3
carrier-bag /'kærɪe 'bæg/ 20/6; 67/15
carrot /'kærət/ 62/5
carry /'kærɪ/ 64/3
cart /kɑːt/ 40/26
carton /'kɑːtn/ 67/1
cartridge /'kɑːtrɪdʒ/ 45/11
case /keɪs/ 32/4; 67/17
cash-desk /'kæʃ desk/ 20/4

cashier /'kæʃɪə(r)/ 20/2
cash-register /'kæʃ redʒɪstə(r)/ 20/3
Caspian Sea /,kæspɪən 'siː/ 6/24
castle /'kɑːsl/ 52/4
cat /kæt/ 56/15
catch /kætʃ/ 64/4
catcher /'kætʃə(r)/ 48/1
caterpillar /'kætəpɪlə(r)/ 59/27
cauliflower /'kɒlɪflaʊə(r)/ 62/10
cedar /'siːdə(r)/ 63/23
ceiling /'siːlɪŋ/ 29/1.
cell /sel/ 16/15
cello /'tʃeləʊ/ 49/8
cement /sɪ'ment/ 23/16
ce'ment-mixer 23/21
centigrade /'sentɪgreɪd/ 70/C
centimetre /'sentɪmiːtə(r)/ 80
centipede /'sentɪpiːd/ 58/22
centre /'sentə(r)/ 47/18, 22; 68/20
century /'sentʃərɪ/ 80
chain /tʃeɪn/ 28/7; 40/18
chair /tʃeə(r)/ 17/15; 29/8, 24; 35/19
chalet /'ʃæleɪ/ 35/8
‡chalk /tʃɔːk/ 18/4
chameleon /kə'miːlɪən/ 59/3
cheek /tʃiːk/ 9/5
‡cheese /tʃiːz/ 20/9
cherry /'tʃerɪ/ 61/7
‡chess /tʃes/ 52/A
'chessmen 52/1
chest /tʃest/ 8/14
chest-of-drawers /,tʃest əv 'drɔːz/ 32/15
chick /tʃɪk/ 36/35
chicken /'tʃɪkɪn/ 36/33
children /'tʃɪldrən/ 71/2
chimney /'tʃɪmnɪ/ 26/2; 37/7
chin /tʃɪn/ 9/6
China Sea /,tʃaɪnə 'siː/ 7/31, 32
chisel /'tʃɪzl/ 24/4
choke /tʃəʊk/ 38/15
chop /tʃɒp/ 66/23
chopper /'tʃɒpə(r)/ 24/15
cigarette /,sɪgə'ret/ 51/8
cinema /'sɪnəmə/ 50/17
circle /'sɜːkl/ 5/2, 6; 50/10; 68/E
circumference /sə'kʌmfərəns/ 68/18
clap /klæp/ 66/17
clarinet /,klærɪ'net/ 49/2
claw /klɔː/ 58/18; 60/3
clean /kliːn/ 74/3
clerk /klɑːk/ 22/1; 54/4
cliff /klɪf/ 35/6
climb /klaɪm/ 64/5
clip /klɪp/ 21/9
clock /klɒk/ 28/24; 32/24
'clock-face 70/4
closed /kləʊzd/ 74/4
cloth /klɒθ/ 30/29, 32; 51/30; 53/13
†clothes /kləʊðz/ 10–13; 32/17
cloud /klaʊd/ 27/2
clown /klaʊn/ 54/13
club /klʌb/ 52/11
clutch /klʌtʃ/ 38/20
coach /kəʊtʃ/ 39/17; 41/4
coastline /'kəʊstlaɪn/ 5/11
coat /kəʊt/ 11/14; 13/9
cobweb /'kɒbweb/ 58/26
cock /kɒk/ 36/34
cockpit /'kɒkpɪt/ 45/22
cockroach /'kɒkrəʊtʃ/ 59/14
‡cocoa /'kəʊkəʊ/ 63/4
coconut /'kəʊkənʌt/ 61/9
cocoon /kə'kuːn/ 59/28
‡coffee /'kɒfɪ/ 63/5
cog /kɒg/ 40/19
coil /kɔɪl/ 59/7
coin /kɔɪn/ 20/25
colander /'kʌləndə(r)/ 30/25
cold /kəʊld/ 33/3; 74/15
collar /'kɒlə(r)/ 11/2
'collar-bone 8/2
collector /kə'lektə(r)/ 41/16
colour /'kʌlə(r)/ 79
comb /kəʊm/ 32/21; 66/12
combine harvester /,kɒmbaɪn 'hɑːvɪstə(r)/
  36/16
comet /'kɒmɪt/ 4/1
compact /'kɒmpækt/ 12/13
compartment /kəm'pɑːtmənt/ 41/5
compass /'kʌmpəs/ 5/C
†compasses /'kʌmpəsɪz/ 18/11
concrete-mixer /'kɒnkriːt mɪksə(r)/ 23/21
conductor /kən'dʌktə(r)/ 15/27; 49/10

cone /kəʊn/ 63/21; 68/23
Congo /ˈkɒŋgəʊ/ 7/50
consonant /ˈkɒnsənənt/ 81
constellation /ˌkɒnstəˈleɪʃn/ 4/2
container /kənˈteɪnə(r)/ 67
continent /ˈkɒntɪnənt/ 6/A
control-panel /kənˈtrəʊl pænl/ 45/28
control tower /kənˈtrəʊl taʊə(r)/ 44/20
convertible /kənˈvɜːtəbl/ 38/38
cooker /ˈkʊkə(r)/ 30/1
cookery-book /ˈkʊkərɪ bʊk/ 30/24
cooling tower /ˈkuːlɪŋ taʊə(r)/ 37/8
Coral Sea /ˌkɒrəl ˈsiː/ 6/29
cord /kɔːd/ 28/28
core /kɔː(r)/ 61/4
cork /kɔːk/ 51/25
corkscrew /ˈkɔːkskruː/ 51/11
corn /kɔːn/ 63/1
corner /ˈkɔːnə(r)/ 69/3
cot /kɒt/ 32/26
‡cotton /ˈkɒtn/ 53/8; 63/6; 73/9
couch /kaʊtʃ/ 29/21
counter /ˈkaʊntə(;r)/ 20/22; 22/3; 50/24
country /ˈkʌntrɪ/ 34
coupé /ˈkuːpeɪ/ 38/39
court /kɔːt/ 16/C; 48/23
cousin /ˈkʌzn/ 71/9
cover /ˈkʌvə(r)/ 52/16
cow /kaʊ/ 36/21
ˈcowshed 36/3
crab /kræb/ 58/17
crane /kreɪn/ 23/1; 42/4
crash-helmet /ˈkræʃ helmɪt/ 40/27
crate /kreɪt/ 67/11
crawl /krɔːl/ 64/6
cream /kriːm/ 12/18
crease /kriːs/ 48/17
crescent /ˈkresnt/ 4/11
crest /krest/ 60/12
‡cricket /ˈkrɪkɪt/ 48/B; 59/11
crocodile /ˈkrɒkədaɪl/ 59/1
crook /krʊk/ 36/27
crooked /ˈkrʊkɪd/ 74/5
crutch /krʌtʃ/ 17/26
cry /kraɪ/ 64/7
crystal /ˈkrɪstl/ 19/17
cube /kjuːb/ 68/24
cucumber /ˈkjuːkʌmbə(r)/ 62/8
cuff /kʌf/ 11/3
cup /kʌp/ 30/1
cupboard /ˈkʌbəd/ 32/13
curtain /ˈkɜːtn/ 26/14; 29/7; 50/6
curve /kɜːv/ 68/3
cushion /ˈkʊʃn/ 29/9
customer /ˈkʌstəmə(r)/ 20/5; 51/22
†customs /ˈkʌstəmz/ 44/1, 2
ˈcustoms-officer 44/2
cut /kʌt/ 64/8
cycle /ˈsaɪkl/ 40/1
cylinder /ˈsɪlɪndə(r)/ 68/25
ˈcylinder-head 38/36
†cymbals /ˈsɪmblz/ 49/29

daffodil /ˈdæfədɪl/ 62/17
daisy /ˈdeɪzɪ/ 62/18
dam /dæm/ 37/2
dance /dɑːns/ 64/9
Danube /ˈdænjuːb/ 7/47
dark /dɑːk/ 75/11
dashboard /ˈdæʃbɔːd/ 38/12
date /deɪt/ 61/10; 70/B
daughter /ˈdɔːtə(r)/ 71/3
daughter-in-law /ˈdɔːtər ɪn lɔː/ 71/7
day /deɪ/ 80
December /dɪˈsembə(r)/ 80
decimal /ˈdesɪml/ 69/21
deck /dek/ 43/19
ˈdeckchair 35/19
deep /diːp/ 74/6
ˌdeep-ˈfreeze 20/14
defence /dɪˈfens/ 45
defendant /dɪˈfendənt/ 16/20
defender /dɪˈfendə(r)/ 47/15, 16
degree /dɪˈgriː/ 70/C
delta /ˈdeltə/ 5/9
dental nurse /ˈdentl nɜːs/ 17/14
dentist /ˈdentɪst/ 17/16 ˋ
depth /depθ/ 69/10
derrick /ˈderɪk/ 37/10
desert /ˈdezət/ 7/E
desk /desk/ 18/7; 21/1; 50/24
‡detection /dɪˈtekʃn/ 16/A
diagonal /daɪˈægənl/ 68/15

dial /ˈdaɪəl/ 19/5; 28/27
diameter /daɪˈæmɪtə(r)/ 68/19
diamond /ˈdaɪəmənd/ 52/12
diary /ˈdaɪərɪ/ 21/5
difficult /ˈdɪfɪkəlt/ 74/12
dig /dɪg/ 64/10
dining-table /ˈdaɪnɪŋ teɪbl/ 29/23
diphthong /ˈdɪfθɒŋ/ 81
directory /dɪˈrektərɪ/ 28/29
dirty /ˈdɜːtɪ/ 74/3
dish /dɪʃ/ 29/32
dish-cloth 30/29
distributor /dɪˈstrɪbjʊtə(r)/ 38/34
dive /daɪv/ 64/11
divide by /dɪˈvaɪd baɪ/ 69/18
dock /dɒk/ 16/21; 42/12
docker /ˈdɒkə(r)/ 54/6
doctor /ˈdɒktə(r)/ 17/21; 55/8
dog /dɒg/ 16/6; 36/28; 56/13
doll /dɒl/ 32/31
dolphin /ˈdɒlfɪn/ 57/3
donkey /ˈdɒŋkɪ/ 56/10
door /dɔː(r)/ 26/7; 28/1
ˈdoorstep 28/4
double bass /ˌdʌbl ˈbeɪs/ 49/9
dove /dʌv/ 60/24
down /daʊn/ 76/4
ˌdownˈstairs 28/21
dragonfly /ˈdrægənflaɪ/ 59/19
drain /dreɪn/ 14/11
draining-board /ˈdreɪnɪŋ bɔːd/ 30/8
ˈdrainpipe 26/17
draw /drɔː/ 64/12
drawer /drɔː(r)/ 32/15
dream /driːm/ 64/14
dress /dres/ 13/8
dressing-gown /ˈdresɪŋ gaʊn/ 10/3
dressing-table /ˈdresɪŋ teɪbl/ 32/10
dressmaker /ˈdresmeɪkə(r)/ 54/10
drill /drɪl/ 17/17; 23/23; 25/3, 4
drink /drɪŋk/ 51/13; 64/13
drive /draɪv/ 64/15
driver /ˈdraɪvə(r)/ 41/2; 54/12
drown /draʊn/ 64/16
drum /drʌm/ 49/30
dry /draɪ/ 74/7
ˈdrying-up cloth 30/32
duck /dʌk/ 36/32
duckling /ˈdʌklɪŋ/ 36/31
dummy /ˈdʌmɪ/ 32/28
dumper-truck /ˈdʌmpə trʌk/ 23/22
dustbin /ˈdʌstbɪn/ 67/8
duster /ˈdʌstə(r)/ 18/5; 31/7
dust-jacket /ˈdʌst dʒækɪt/ 52/17
dustpan /ˈdʌstpæn/ 31/8

eagle /ˈiːgl/ 60/2
ear /ɪə(r)/ 9/3; 63/2
ˈear-ring 12/10
‡Earth /ɜːθ/ 4/7
easel /ˈiːzl/ 18/3
east /iːst/ 5/C
ˌEast ˌChina ˈSea 7/32
easy /ˈiːzɪ/ 74/12
eat /iːt/ 64/17
eclipse /ɪˈklɪps/ 4/10
edge /edʒ/ 69/4
‡education /ˌedjuˈkeɪʃn/ 18–19
eel /iːl/ 58/10
egg /eg/ 20/11
ˈeggplant 62/16
eight /eɪt/ 80
eighteen /ˌeɪˈtiːn/ 80
eighth /eɪtθ/ 80
eighty /ˈeɪtɪ/ 80
‡elastic /ɪˈlæstɪk/ 53/7
elbow /ˈelbəʊ/ 8/23
electric /ɪˈlektrɪk/ 25/4; 49/26
electrician /ˌɪlekˈtrɪʃn/ 55/2
elephant /ˈelɪfənt/ 57/21
eleven /ɪˈlevn/ 80
ellipse /ɪˈlɪps/ 68/F
empty /ˈemptɪ/ 74/8
engine /ˈendʒɪn/ 17/7; 38/31; 41/3; 44/12
envelope /ˈenvələʊp/ 21/11; 22/14
equal /ˈiːkwəl/ 69/19
Equator /ɪˈkweɪtə(r)/ 5/4
escape /ɪˈskeɪp/ 17/10
estate /ɪˈsteɪt/ 38/40
estuary /ˈestjʊərɪ/ 5/10
Europe /ˈjʊərəp/ 6/3
excavator /ˈekskəveɪtə(r)/ 23/20
exercise-book /ˈeksəsaɪz bʊk/ 18/18

exhaust(-pipe) /ɪgˈzɔːst paɪp/ 38/7; 40/35
extinguisher /ɪkˈstɪŋgwɪʃə(r)/ 17/6
eye /aɪ/ 9/1; 9/D; 53/23
ˈeyeball 9/15
ˈeyebrow 9/16
ˈeyelash 9/18
ˈeyelid 9/17
‡ˈeye-shadow 12/17

face /feɪs/ 9/C; 70/4
‡ˈface-cream 12/18
(ˈface-)flannel 33/17
Fahrenheit /ˈfærənhaɪt/ 70/C
fall /fɔːl/ 64/18
family /ˈfæməlɪ/ 71
fan /fæn/ 21/14
farm /fɑːm/ 36
farmer /ˈfɑːmə(r)/ 36/15
ˈfarmhouse 36/7
ˈfarmyard 36/6
fast /fɑːst/ 74/9
fastener /ˈfɑːsnə(r)/ 53/22
fat /fæt/ 74/10
father /ˈfɑːðə(r)/ 71/4
father-in-law /ˈfɑːðər ɪn lɔː/ 71/6
feather /ˈfeðə(r)/ 60/5
February /ˈfebrʊərɪ/ 80
feeler /ˈfiːlə(r)/ 59/16
fence /fens/ 36/17
fern /fɜːn/ 61/32
ferry /ˈferɪ/ 43/15
field /fiːld/ 34/13; 36/8; 47/6
fielder /ˈfiːldə(r)/ 48/15
fifteen /ˌfɪfˈtiːn/ 80
fifth /fɪfθ/ 80
fifty /ˈfɪftɪ/ 80
fig /fɪg/ 61/29
fight /ˌfaɪt/ 64/19
fighter plane /ˈfaɪtə pleɪn/ 45/21
figure /ˈfɪgə(r)/ 68/G
file /faɪl/ 12/12; 21/18; 24/2
filing-cabinet /ˈfaɪlɪŋ kæbɪnət/ 21/19
film /fɪlm/ 52/24
fin /fɪn/ 44/13; 57/4; 58/2
finger /ˈfɪŋgə(r)/ 8/30
ˈfingerprint 16/11
fir /fɜː(r)/ 63/20
fire /ˈfaɪə(r)/ 17/11; 29/6
ˈfire brigade 17/A
ˈfire-engine 17/7
ˈfire-escape 17/10
ˈfire-extinguisher 17/6
ˈfireman 17/1
ˈfireplace 29/4
first /fɜːst/ 75/10; 80
fish /fɪʃ/ 58
fisherman /ˈfɪʃəmən/ 48/18
fishing /ˈfɪʃɪŋ/ 48/C
fist /fɪst/ 8/26
five /faɪv/ 80
flag /flæg/ 41/11
flame /fleɪm/ 17/13
flamingo /fləˈmɪŋgəʊ/ 60/8
flannel /ˈflænl/ 33/17
flap /flæp/ 22/15
flask /flɑːsk/ 19/16; 67/9
flat /flæt/ 15/19
fleet /fliːt/ 72/4
‡flex /fleks/ 31/12
flight /flaɪt/ 72/5
flipper /ˈflɪpə(r)/ 35/21; 57/10
flock /flɒk/ 72/6
floor /flɔː(r)/ 28/11
florist /ˈflɒrɪst/ 55/5
flower /ˈflaʊə(r)/ 27/20; 62
ˈflower-bed 27/21
ˈflower-pot 27/24
fluke /fluːk/ 57/2
flute /fluːt/ 49/1
fly /flaɪ/ 59/23; 64/20
ˈfly-over 39/2
foal /fəʊl/ 56/2
foot /fʊt/ 8/37; 60/9
‡football 47/A
ˈfootbrake 38/19
‡ˈfootlights 50/13
ˈfootpath 34/10
ˈfootprint 16/12
ˈfootrest 40/37
forearm /ˈfɔːrɑːm/ 8/24
forehead /ˈfɒrɪd/ 9/8
forest /ˈfɒrɪst/ 34/9
fork /fɔːk/ 24/10; 27/25; 29/26
ˌfork-lift ˈtruck 42/17

84

forty /ˈfɔːtɪ/ 80
forward /ˈfɔːwəd/ 47/22
†foundations /faʊnˈdeɪʃnz/ 23/10
four /fɔː(r)/ 80
fourteen /ˌfɔːˈtiːn/ 80
fourth /fɔːθ/ 80
fox /fɒks/ 56/24
fraction /ˈfrækʃn/ 69/22
frame /freɪm/ 26/9; 29/13
freezer /ˈfriːzə(r)/ 20/14
Friday /ˈfraɪdɪ/ 80
fridge /frɪdʒ/ 30/5
frill /frɪl/ 53/14
frog /frɒg/ 58/20
from /frɒm/ 77/3, 11
frond /frɒnd/ 61/33
front /frʌnt/ 69/7; 76/7
ˌfront ˈdoor 26/7
frown /fraʊn/ 66/14
‡fruit /fruːt/ 20/17; 61
ˈfruit-tree 36/11
frying-pan /ˈfraɪɪŋ pæn/ 30/11
‡fuel /ˈfjʊəl/ 37/9
full /fʊl/ 4/13; 74/8
funnel /ˈfʌnl/ 42/9; 43/21
furrow /ˈfʌrəʊ/ 36/20
fuselage /ˈfjuːzəlɑːʒ/ 44/10

galaxy /ˈgæləksɪ/ 4/3
gallery /ˈgælərɪ/ 50/9
gang /gæŋ/ 72/7
Ganges /ˈgændʒiːz/ 7/52
gangway /ˈgæŋweɪ/ 42/10; 50/21
gaol /dʒeɪl/ 16/B
garage /ˈgærɑːʒ/ 26/6
garden /ˈgɑːdn/ 24/10; 26/20; 27
gardener /ˈgɑːdnə(r)/ 55/3
gate /geɪt/ 27/16
gauge /geɪdʒ/ 38/13
gear-lever /ˈgɪə liːvə(r)/ 38/21; 40/38
gill /gɪl/ 58/5
giraffe /dʒɪˈrɑːf/ 57/15
girl /gɜːl/ 12
give /gɪv/ 66/11
glass /glɑːs/ 29/29; 51/26
†glasses /ˈglɑːsɪz/ 11/23
glider /ˈglaɪdə(r)/ 44/14
globe /gləʊb/ 5/A
glove /glʌv/ 11/20; 46/12; 48/3
‡glue /gluː/ 18/13
goal /gəʊl/ 46/25; 47/7, 8, 9
ˈgoalkeeper 47/14
ˈgoal-line 47/8
goat /gəʊt/ 36/24
Gobi /ˈgəʊbɪ/ 7/44
†goggles /ˈgɒglz/ 35/15; 40/28
good /gʊd/ 75/8
ˈgoods-truck 41/28
goose /guːs/ 60/25
gorilla /gəˈrɪlə/ 57/14
gown /gaʊn/ 16/24
gram /græm/ 80
granddaughter /ˈgrænˌdɔːtə(r)/ 71/12
grandson /ˈgrænsʌn/ 71/12
grape /greɪp/ 61/12
‡†grapefruit /ˈgreɪpfruːt/ 61/30
grass /grɑːs/ 26/21
grasshopper /ˈgrɑːshɒpə(r)/ 59/12
green /griːn/ 79
greengrocer /ˈgriːngrəʊsə(r)/ 55/1
grenade /grɪˈneɪd/ 45/9
grey /greɪ/ 79
grill /grɪl/ 30/3; 38/27
groundnut /ˈgraʊndnʌt/ 61/11
groundsheet /ˈgraʊndʃiːt/ 35/2
guard /gɑːd/ 41/10
guided missile /ˌgaɪdɪd ˈmɪsaɪl/ 45/4
Guinea (Gulf of) /ˈgɪnɪ/ 6/19
guitar /gɪˈtɑː(r)/ 49/26
gulf /gʌlf/ 6/C
gull /gʌl/ 60/21
gum /gʌm/ 18/13
gun /gʌn/ 45/6, 15
gutter /ˈgʌtə(r)/ 14/10; 26/16
gym-shoe /ˈdʒɪm ʃuː/ 10/15

hacksaw /ˈhæksɔː/ 25/18
hair /heə(r)/ 8/9
ˈhairbrush 32/20
ˈhairdresser 54/1
ˈhairdrier 31/14
half /hɑːf/ 4/12; 47/17, 18, 19; 69/12
ˌhalfway ˈline 47/13
hall /hɔːl/ 28; 44/1

hammer /ˈhæmə(r)/ 25/14
hand /hænd/ 8/27; 70/1, 2, 3
ˈhandbag 13/16; 67/5
ˈhandbrake 38/22
†ˈhandcuffs 16/8
ˈhand-drill 25/3
ˈhand-grenade 45/9
handkerchief /ˈhæŋkətʃɪf/ 13/14
handle /ˈhændl/ 25/16; 29/38; 33/8
†ˈhandle-bars 40/6
ˈhandrail 28/19
hangar /ˈhæŋə(r)/ 44/21
hanger /ˈhæŋə(r)/ 32/19
happy /ˈhæpɪ/ 74/11
hard /hɑːd/ 74/12, 13
‡harness /ˈhɑːnɪs/ 40/23
hat /hæt/ 11/13; 13/4
hawk /hɔːk/ 60/6
hay /heɪ/ 36/2
ˈhayloft 36/1
he /hiː/ 79
head /hed/ 8/10; 25/15
ˈheadboard 32/2
ˈheadlamp 40/5
ˈheadlight 38/29
heap /hiːp/ 72/9
heart /hɑːt/ 9/23; 52/13
heavy /ˈhevɪ/ 75/12
hedge /hedʒ/ 27/17; 34/14
hedgehog /ˈhedʒhɒg/ 56/26
heel /hiːl/ 9/38; 11/11
height /haɪt/ 69/9
helicopter /ˈhelɪkɒptə(r)/ 44/15
helmet /ˈhelmɪt/ 16/2; 17/2; 40/27
hem /hem/ 53/4
hen /hen/ 36/33
her /hɜː(r)/ 79
herd /hɜːd/ 72/10
here /hɪə(r)/ 79
heron /ˈherən/ 60/15
herring /ˈherɪŋ/ 58/6
hers /hɜːz/ 79
†hibiscus /hɪˈbɪskəs/ 62/24
high /haɪ/ 74/14
hill /hɪl/ 34/10
him /hɪm/ 79
Himalayas /ˌhɪməˈleɪəz/ 7/40
hinge /hɪndʒ/ 28/9
hip /hɪp/ 8/18
ˈhip-bone 8/7
hippopotamus /ˌhɪpəˈpɒtəməs/ 57/20
his /hɪz/ 79
hit /hɪt/ 66/5
hobby /ˈhɒbɪ/ 52
‡hockey /ˈhɒkɪ/ 46/D
hod /hɒd/ 23/18
hold /həʊld/ 42/8; 66/20
holdall /ˈhəʊldɔːl/ 67/18
hole /həʊl/ 33/5; 53/16
ˈhole-punch 21/6
hollow /ˈhɒləʊ/ 75/14
hook /hʊk/ 48/21; 53/23
hoover /ˈhuːvə(r)/ 31/1
horizon /həˈraɪzn/ 42/1
horn /hɔːn/ 49/14; 56/9; 57/26
horse /hɔːs/ 40/21; 46/2; 56/1
‡ˈhorse-racing 46/A
hosepipe /ˈhəʊzpaɪp/ 17/3
hospital /ˈhɒspɪtl/ 17/C
hot /hɒt/ 33/2; 74/15
hotel /həʊˈtel/ 35/7
hour /ˈaʊə(r)/ 70/2; 80
house /haʊs/ 26; 37/3
ˈhousehold 31
‡hovercraft /ˈhɒvəkrɑːft/ 42/18
hubcap /ˈhʌbkæp/ 38/30
Hudson Bay /ˌhʌdsn ˈbeɪ/ 6/16
hug /hʌg/ 66/6
human /ˈhjuːmən/ 8–9
humming-bird /ˈhʌmɪŋ bɜːd/ 60/27
hump /hʌmp/ 56/7
hundred /ˈhʌndrəd/ 80
husband /ˈhʌzbənd/ 71/1
Huang He /hwæŋ/ 7/54
hydrant /ˈhaɪdrənt/ 17/5
hypotenuse /haɪˈpɒtənjuːz/ 68/12

I /aɪ/ 79
ice-cream /ˌaɪs ˈkriːm/ 35/17
icicle /ˈaɪsɪkl/ 27/8
ignition /ɪgˈnɪʃn/ 38/14
illustration /ˌɪləˈstreɪʃn/ 52/20
in /ɪn/ 76/7, 10
index /ˈɪndeks/ 50/23

Indian /ˈɪndɪən/ 6/13
indicator /ˈɪndɪkeɪtə(r)/ 38/5
Indus /ˈɪndəs/ 71/51
insect /ˈɪnsekt/ 59/B
inside /ˌɪnˈsaɪd/ 47/21, 23; 76/10
ˌinside ˈlane 39/6
insides /ˌɪnˈsaɪdz/ 9/E
inspector /ɪnˈspektə(r)/ 41/6
instep /ˈɪnstep/ 9/39
intestines /ɪnˈtestɪnz/ 9/27
into /ˈɪntʊ/ 76/9
iris /ˈaɪərɪs/ 9/20
iron /ˈaɪən/ 31/11; 66/18
ironing-board /ˈaɪənɪŋ bɔːd/ 31/3
‡irrigation /ɪrɪˈgeɪʃn/ 36/17
island /ˈaɪlənd/ 5/12
it /ɪt/ 79
its /ɪts/ 79

jack /dʒæk/ 52/11
jacket /ˈdʒækɪt/ 10/8; 52/17
jail /dʒeɪl/ 16/B
January /ˈdʒænjʊərɪ/ 80
Japan (Sea of) /dʒəˈpæn/ 7/33
jaw /dʒɔː/ 9/9
†jeans /dʒiːnz/ 10/7
jeep /dʒiːp/ 45/5
jelly-fish /ˈdʒelɪ fɪʃ/ 58/11
jersey /ˈdʒɜːzɪ/ 13/5
jet /dʒet/ 44/12
‡jewellery /ˈdʒuːəlrɪ/ 32/23
jockey /ˈdʒɒkɪ/ 46/1
†jodhpurs /ˈdʒɒdpəz/ 46/8
joint /dʒɔɪnt/ 73/4
judge /dʒʌdʒ/ 16/22
‡judo /ˈdʒuːdəʊ/ 46/G
ˈjudo suit 46/23
jug /dʒʌg/ 29/37; 30/20
juke-box /ˈdʒuːk bɒks/ 51/15
July /dʒuˈlaɪ/ 80
jump /dʒʌmp/ 64/21
jumper /ˈdʒʌmpə(r)/ 10/6; 13/5
June /dʒuːn/ 80
junk /dʒʌŋk/ 43/5
jury /ˈdʒʊərɪ/ 16/17

Kalahari /kæləˈhɑːrɪ/ 7/42
kangaroo /ˌkæŋgəˈruː/ 57/6
keeper /ˈkiːpə(r)/ 47/14; 48/11
kerb /kɜːb/ 14/9
kernel /ˈkɜːnl/ 61/28
kettle /ˈketl/ 30/13
key /kiː/ 28/15; 49/16
keyhole /ˈkiːhəʊl/ 28/6
kick /kɪk/ 64/22
kidney /ˈkɪdnɪ/ 9/26
kilogram /ˈkɪləgræm/ 80
kilometre /ˈkɪləmiːtə(r)/ 80
king /kɪŋ/ 52/8, 13
kingfisher /ˈkɪŋfɪʃə(r)/ 60/30
kiss /kɪs/ 66/7
kitchen /ˈkɪtʃɪn/ 30
kite /kaɪt/ 35/30
kitten /ˈkɪtn/ 56/16
knave /neɪv/ 52/11
knee /niː/ 8/34
kneecap /ˈniːkæp/ 8/8
kneel /niːl/ 64/23
knife /naɪf/ 24/5; 29/28, 41
knight /naɪt/ 52/5
knitting /ˈnɪtɪŋ/ 53/21
ˈknitting-needle 53/18
knocker /ˈnɒkə(r)/ 28/2

lab /læb/ 19
label /ˈleɪbl/ 22/22
laboratory /ləˈbɒrətrɪ/ 19
‡lace /leɪs/ 53/9
ladder /ˈlædə(r)/ 17/8; 23/5
ladle /ˈleɪdl/ 30/31
lake /leɪk/ 5/13; 34/5
lamb /læm/ 36/30
lamp /læmp/ 29/15; 32/25
ˈlamp-post 15/24
ˈlamp-shade 29/16
lane /leɪn/ 39/5, 6
lapel /ləˈpel/ 11/15
larder /ˈlɑːdə(r)/ 30/6
large /lɑːdʒ/ 74/1
last /lɑːst/ 75/10
latitude /ˈlætɪtjuːd/ 5/15
laugh /lɑːf/ 64/24
launch /lɔːntʃ/ 43/12
launching-pad /ˈlɔːntʃɪŋ pæd/ 4/17

laundry-basket /'lɔːndrɪ bɑːskɪt/ 33/26
lavatory /'lævətrɪ/ 33/7
law /lɔː/ 16
'law court 16/C
lawn /lɔːn/ 27/19
lawyer /'lɔːjə(r)/ 16/23
leaf /liːf/ 63/15
leap /liːp/ 64/21
leaves /liːvz/ 27/15
ledge /ledʒ/ 26/11
left /left/ 47/15, 17, 20, 21
leg /leg/ 8/32
‡leisure /'leʒə(r)/ 50
lemon /'lemən/ 61/14
length /leŋθ/ 69/11; 80
lens /lenz/ 19/10; 52/26
leopard /'lepəd/ 57/18
letter /'letə(r)/ 22/7, 10
'letter-basket 21/12
'letter-box 14/1; 22/4; 28/5
lettuce /'letɪs/ 62/12
librarian /laɪ'breərɪən/ 50/22
library /'laɪbrərɪ/ 50 /C
lick /lɪk/ 64/25
lid /lɪd/ 29/35
lie /laɪ/ 65/3
light /laɪt/ 14/7; 17/18; 28/22; 38/4, 5, 29;
    40/30; 44/17; 75/11, 12
'light-bulb 31/13
‡lightning /'laɪtnɪŋ/ 27/1
'light-switch 28/13
line /laɪn/ 5/14, 15; 27/28; 47/8, 12, 13;
    48/20, 26; 68/A; 73/5
liner /'laɪnə(r)/ 43/20
linesman /'laɪnzmən/ 47/2
'line-up 47/C
lion /'laɪən/ 57/16
lip /lɪp/ 9/13
'lipstick 12/19
liquid /'lɪkwɪd/ 30/28; 80
listen /'lɪsn/ 65/1
litre /'liːtə(r)/ 80
litter-bin/-basket /'lɪtə(r)/ 15/30
little /'lɪtl/ 74/1
liver /'lɪvə(r)/ 9/25
living-room /'lɪvɪŋ rʊm/ 29
lizard /'lɪzəd/ 59/9
llama /'lɑːmə/ 56/5
loaf /ləʊf/ 73/6
lobster /'lɒbstə(r)/ 58/12
lock /lɒk/ 28/7
locust /'ləʊkəst/ 59/10
log /lɒg/ 63/18
long /lɒŋ/ 74/16
longitude /'lɒndʒɪtjuːd/ 5/14
loo /luː/ 33/7
loose /luːs/ 75/16
lorry /'lɒrɪ/ 14/15; 39/14
loud /laʊd/ 75/13
loudspeaker /ˌlaʊd'spiːkə(r)/ 49/28
low /ləʊ/ 74/14
‡luggage /'lʌgɪdʒ/ 44/4
'luggage-rack 41/9
lump /lʌmp/ 73/7
lung /lʌŋ/ 9/24
lychee /ˌlaɪ'tʃiː/ 61/26

mac /mæk/ 11/12
machine /mə'ʃiːn/ 31/4; 53/1
ma'chine-gun 45/15
mackintosh /'mækɪntɒʃ/ 11/12
magnet /'mægnɪt/ 19/19
magnifying-glass /'mægnɪfaɪɪŋ glɑːs/ 16/10
mailbag /'meɪlbæg/ 22/6
‡maize /meɪz/ 63/1
mallet /'mælɪt/ 25/1
man /mæn/ 10–11
mane /meɪn/ 57/17
mango /'mæŋgəʊ/ 61/15
mantelpiece /'mæntlpiːs/ 29/5
mantis /'mæntɪs/ 59/15
map /mæp/ 5/B; 18/21
March /mɑːtʃ/ 80
market /'mɑːkɪt/ 14/3
marrow /'mærəʊ/ 62/7
‡mascara /mæ'skɑːrə/ 12/14
mask /mɑːsk/ 35/15; 48/2
mast /mɑːst/ 43/3
mat /mæt/ 26/18; 28/10; 29/25; 33/23
match /mætʃ/ 51/16
'matchbox 51/5
material /mə'tɪərɪəl/ 53/13
mattock /'mætək/ 23/19

mattress /'mætrɪs/ 32/8
May /meɪ/ 80
me /miː/ 79
meadow /'medəʊ/ 34/11
measure /'meʒə(r)/ 53/25; 80
measurement /'meʒəmənt/ 69
‡meat /miːt/ 20/13
mechanic /mɪ'kænɪk/ 54/5
medical /'medɪkl/ 17
medicine /'medsɪn/ 17/30
Mediterranean /ˌmedɪtə'reɪnɪən/ 6/22
Mekong /miː'kɒŋ/ 7/53
menu /'menjuː/ 51/23
meter /'miːtə(r)/ 19/4
metre /'miːtə(r)/ 80
Mexico (Gulf of) /'meksɪkəʊ/ 6/17
microphone /'maɪkrəfəʊn/ 49/25
microscope /'maɪkrəskəʊp/ 19/9
midfield /'mɪdfiːld/ 47/17, 18, 19
mike /maɪk/ 49/25
milk /mɪlk/ 20/10
'milk-jug 29/37
millilitre /'mɪlɪliːtə(r)/ 80
millimetre /'mɪlɪmiːtə(r)/ 80
million /'mɪlɪən/ 80
mine /maɪn/ 79
miner /'maɪnə(r)/ 54/7
minus /'maɪnəs/ 69/17
minute /'mɪnɪt/ 70/1; 80
mirror /'mɪrə(r)/ 32/12; 38/1; 40/3
missile /'mɪsaɪl/ 45/4
Mississippi /ˌmɪsɪ'sɪpɪ/ 7/45
mixer /'mɪksə(r)/ 23/21
Monday /'mʌndɪ/ 80
monkey /'mʌŋkɪ/ 57/13
month /mʌnθ/ 80
Moon /muːn/ 4/6
mop /mɒp/ 31/5
mortar /'mɔːtə(r)/ 19/21
mosquito /mə'skiːtəʊ/ 59/20
moth /mɒθ/ 59/26
mother /'mʌðə(r)/ 71/4
mother-in-law /'mʌðər ɪn lɔː/ 71/6
motor /'məʊtə(r)/ 43/13
'motorbike/'motorcycle 14/17; 39/20
'motor-boat 35/34; 43/12
'motor-car 38
'motor-launch 43/12
'motorway 39/1
mountain /'maʊntɪn/ 34/2
'mountain 'range 7
mouse /maʊs/ 56/18
moustache /mə'stɑːʃ/ 9/10
mouth /maʊθ/ 9/4; 58/8
'mouthpiece 49/23
mudguard /'mʌdgɑːd/ 40/10
mug /mʌg/ 51/3
multiply by /'mʌltɪplaɪ/ 69/16
muscle /'mʌsl/ 9/31
mushroom /'mʌʃrʊm/ 62/14
‡music /'mjuːzɪk/ 49
musician /mjuː'zɪʃn/ 49/3
‡mustard /'mʌstəd/ 51/28
my /maɪ/ 79

nail /neɪl/ 8/31; 25/11
'nail-brush 33/18
'nail-file 12/12
‡'nail-polish 12/15
‡'nail-varnish 12/15
napkin /'næpkɪn/ 51/31
nappy /'næpɪ/ 32/36
narrow /'nærəʊ/ 75/1
national /'næʃənl/ 45
navigator /'nævɪgeɪtə(r)/ 45/26
Navy /'neɪvɪ/ 45/B
near /nɪə(r)/ 76/15
neck /nek/ 8/11
necklace /'neklɪs/ 12/11
needle /'niːdl/ 5/16; 19/6; 53/6, 18; 63/22
negative /'negətɪv/ 52/23
nephew /'nevjuː/ 71/11
nest /nest/ 60/29
net /net/ 46/20; 48/24
new /njuː/ 4/11; 75/3
,new 'moon 4/11
next /nekst/ 76/14
niece /niːs/ 71/11
Niger /'naɪdʒə(r)/ 7/49
nightdress /'naɪtdres/ 12/6
'nightgown 12/6
Nile /naɪl/ 7/48
nine /naɪn/ 80

nineteen /naɪn'tiːn/ 80
ninety /'naɪntɪ/ 80
ninth /naɪnθ/ 80
north /nɔːθ/ 5/C
northeast /ˌnɔːθ'iːst/ 5/C
,North 'Pole 5/1
,North 'Sea 6/20
northwest /ˌnɔːθ'west/ 5/C
nose /nəʊz/ 9/2
nosecone /'nəʊzkəʊn/ 4/15
note /nəʊt/ 20/24
'notebook 21/23
'notepad 21/23
nothing /'nʌθɪŋ/ 80
noun /naʊn/ 72–73
nought /nɔːt/ 80
November /nəʊ'vembə(r)/ 80
nozzle /'nɒzl/ 17/4
number /'nʌmbə(r)/ 41/21; 80
'number-plate 38/28
nurse /nɜːs/ 17/14, 25; 55/10
nut /nʌt/ 25/13; 61/11, 27

oak /əʊk/ 63/10
oar /ɔː(r)/ 43/7
object /'ɒbdʒɪkt/ 31
oblong /'ɒblɒŋ/ 68/D
obtuse /əb'tjuːs/ 68/10
occupation /ˌɒkjʊ'peɪʃn/ 54–55
ocean /'əʊʃn/ 6/B
o'clock /ə'klɒk/ 70/5
October /ɒk'təʊbə(r)/ 80
octopus /'ɒktəpəs/ 58/23
off /ɒf/ 77/6
office /'ɒfɪs/ 21; 41/14
'office-block 15/20
oil-derrick /'ɔɪl derɪk/ 37/10
oil-rig /'ɔɪl rɪg/ 37/11
oil-tanker /'ɔɪl tæŋkə(r)/ 43/18
Okhotsk (Sea of) /əʊ'kɒtsk/ 7/34
old /əʊld/ 4/14; 75/2, 3
olive /'ɒlɪv/ 63/3
on /ɒn/ 76/12
one /wʌn/ 79–80
onion /'ʌnjən/ 62/13
onto /'ɒntə/ 76/13
open /'əʊpən/ 65/2; 74/4
opener /'əʊpnə(r)/ 51/7
operator /'ɒpəreɪtə(r)/ 21/16
optician /ɒp'tɪʃn/ 55/14
orange /'ɒrɪndʒ/ 61/16; 79
orbit /'ɔːbɪt/ 4/9
orchard /'ɔːtʃəd/ 36/12
orchestra /'ɔːkɪstrə/ 49 ; 50/12
orchid /'ɔːkɪd/ 62/21
ostrich /'ɒstrɪtʃ/ 60/1
our /'aʊə(r)/ 79
ours /'aʊəz/ 79
out /aʊt/ 76/11
outboard motor /ˌaʊtbɔːd 'məʊtə(r)/ 43/13
outside /ˌaʊt'saɪd/ 47/20, 24; 76/1
,outside 'lane 39/5
oval /'əʊvl/ 68/F
oven /'ʌvn/ 30/2
over /'əʊvə(r)/ 77/7
overtake /ˌəʊvə'teɪk/ 66/13
owl /aʊl/ 60/7
oyster /'ɔɪstə(r)/ 58/16

Pacific /pə'sɪfɪk/ 6/9, 10
pack /pæk/ 52/10
packet /'pækɪt/ 73/10, 11
pad /pæd/ 21/4, 23; 48/12
paddle /'pædl/ 43/9
page /peɪdʒ/ 52/19
paint /peɪnt/ 18/27; 65/4
'paintbrush 18/25
palette /'pælət/ 18/26
palm /pɑːm/ 8/28; 63/19
pan /pæn/ 19/2; 30/11, 12
pane /pæn/ 26/10
panel /'pænl/ 45/28
pannier /'pænɪə(r)/ 40/34
†pants /pænts/ 10/2; 12/3
papaya /pə'paɪə/ 61/25
paper /'peɪpə(r)/ 21/10, 20; 22/12; 24/3; 33/9
,paper-'bag 67/7
'paper-clip 21/9
parachute /'pærəʃuːt/ 45/25
parallel /'pærəlel/ 68/5
parcel /'pɑːsl/ 22/20
park /pɑːk/ 14/12, 32
parking-meter /'pɑːkɪŋ miːtə(r)/ 15/25

86

parrot /'pærət/ 60/20
party /'pɑːtɪ/ 72/11
pass /pɑːs/ 66/13
passenger /'pæsɪndʒə(r)/ 41/19; 44/6
passport /'pɑːspɔːt/ 44/3
path /pɑːθ/ 27/18; 34/7
patient /'peɪʃnt/ 17/20
patio /'pætɪəʊ/ 26/5
pattern /'pætən/ 53/20
pavement /'peɪvmənt/ 15/29
paw /pɔː/ 56/17
pawn /pɔːn/ 52/3
pawpaw /'pɔːpɔː/ 61/25
pea /piː/ 62/3
peach /piːtʃ/ 61/19
peacock /'piːkɒk/ 60/11
peak /piːk/ 34/3
peanut /'piːnʌt/ 61/11
pear /peə(r)/ 61/22
pebble /'pebl/ 35/28
pedal /'pedl/ 40/17; 49/17
pedestrian crossing /pɪ'destrɪən 'krɒsɪŋ/ 14/2
‡peel /piːl/ 61/3, 18
peg /peg/ 27/30; 28/14
pelvis /'pelvɪs/ 8/7
pen /pen/ 18/17; 36/5
penalty /'penltɪ/ 47/10, 11
pencil /'pensl/ 18/15
penguin /'peŋgwɪn/ 60/13
penknife /'pennaɪf/ 24/5
pepper /'pepə(r)/ 51/29
per cent /pə 'sent/ 69/20
perfume /'pɜːfjuːm/ 12/16
periscope /'perɪskəʊp/ 45/20
perpendicular /ˌpɜːpən'dɪkjʊlə(r)/ 68/4
Persian Gulf /ˌpɜːʃn 'gʌlf/ 6/26
pestle /'pesl/ 19/20
petal /'petl/ 62/20
petrol-cap /'petrəl kæp/ 38/3
'petrol gauge 38/13
'petrol-pump 39/8
'petrol-station 39/7
petticoat /'petɪkəʊt/ 12/2
phase /feɪz/ 4/B
pheasant /'feznt/ 60/14
phone /fəʊn/ 28/25
'phone-box 15/31
phonetic /fə'netɪk/ 81
photo /'fəʊtəʊ/ 52/22
photograph /'fəʊtəgrɑːf/ 52/22
photographer /fə'tɒgrəfə(r)/ 55/4
‡photography /fə'tɒgrəfɪ/ 52/D
piano /pɪ'ænəʊ/ 49/15
pick /pɪk/ 66/8
'pick-axe 23/12
picture /'pɪktʃə(r)/ 29/12
piece /piːs/ 52/1; 73/8
pier /pɪə(r)/ 42/2
pig /pɪg/ 56/3
pigeon /'pɪdʒɪn/ 60/31
pile /paɪl/ 72/11
pill /pɪl/ 17/29
pillar-box /'pɪlə bɒks/ 22/4
pillow /'pɪləʊ/ 32/3
'pillow-case 32/4
'pillow-slip 32/4
pilot /'paɪlət/ 45/27
pin /pɪn/ 30/18; 53/10, 12
pincer /'pɪnsə(r)/ 58/18
†pincers /'pɪnsəz/ 24/14
pineapple /'paɪnæpl/ 61/24
pink /pɪŋk/ 79
pipe /paɪp/ 23/9; 26/17; 40/35
'pipeline 37/12
pistol /'pɪstl/ 45/10
pit /pɪt/ 50/12
pitch /pɪtʃ/ 47/6; 48/13
plane /pleɪn/ 25/2; 44/9; 45/21
planet /'plænɪt/ 4/4
plank /plæŋk/ 23/11
plant /plɑːnt/ 61–63
plate /pleɪt/ 72/13
plateau /'plætəʊ/ 34/1
platform /'plætfɔːm/ 18/6; 41/20, 21
player /'pleɪə(r)/ 29/11; 46/24; 47/17, 18, 19; 49/3
playing-card /'pleɪɪŋ kɑːd/ 52/10
pleat /pliːt/ 53/11
†pliers /'plaɪəz/ 25/19
plimsoll /'plɪmsəl/ 10/15
plough /plaʊ/ 36/19
plug /plʌg/ 31/15; 33/6; 38/35

plug-hole /'plʌg həʊl/ 33/5
plum /plʌm/ 61/23
plus /plʌs/ 69/15
pneumatic drill /njuːˌmætɪk 'drɪl/ 23/23
pocket /'pɒkɪt/ 11/16
pod /pɒd/ 62/4; 63/4
point /pɔɪnt/ 69/21
pointer /'pɔɪntə(r)/ 19/6
†points /pɔɪnts/ 41/26
pole /pəʊl/ 43/11; 47/27
Pole /pəʊl/ 5/1, 7
police /pə'liːs/ 16
po'lice-car 16/5
po'lice-dog 16/6
po'liceman 16/1; 55/13
po'lice-station 16/4
pond /pɒnd/ 34/19; 36/9
pop group /'pɒp gruːp/ 49
porter /'pɔːtə(r)/ 54/14
possessive /pə'zesɪv/ 78
postal order /'pəʊstl ɔːdə(r)/ 22/17
post-box /'pəʊst bɒks/ 22/4
postcard /'pəʊstkɑːd/ 22/13
poster /'pəʊstə(r)/ 18/24
postman /'pəʊstmən/ 22/5
postmark /'pəʊstmɑːk/ 22/8
post office /'pəʊst ɒfɪs/ 22
pot /pɒt/ 29/33; 30/12; 51/28, 29
potato /pə'teɪtəʊ/ 62/6
potty /'pɒtɪ/ 32/32
pouch /paʊtʃ/ 57/7
powder /'paʊdə(r)/ 31/9, 18
'powder-compact 12/13
‡power /'paʊə(r)/ 37
'power-house 37/3
'power-point 31/16
'power station 37/6
pram /præm/ 14/18
preposition /prepə'zɪʃn/ 76–77
press-stud /'pres stʌd/ 53/27
pretty /'prɪtɪ/ 75/9
print /prɪnt/ 52/22
prison /'prɪzn/ 16/B
prisoner /'prɪznə(r)/ 16/14
profession /prə'feʃn/ 54–55
projectionist /prə'dʒekʃənɪst/ 50/16
projection room /prə'dʒekʃn ruːm/ 50/14
projector /prə'dʒektə(r)/ 50/15; 52/29
promenade /ˌprɒmə'nɑːd/ 35/9
pronoun /'prəʊnaʊn/ 78
pronunciation /prɪˌnʌnsɪ'eɪʃn/ 81
propeller /prə'pelə(r)/ 43/14; 44/18
protractor /prə'træktə(r)/ 18/12
pull /pʊl/ 65/5
pullover /'pʊləʊvə(r)/ 13/5
pump /pʌmp/ 40/16; 51/19
punch pʌntʃ/ 21/6
punt /pʌnt/ 43/10
pupil /'pjuːpl/ 9/19; 18/8
puppy /'pʌpɪ/ 56/14
purple /'pɜːpl/ 79
purse /pɜːs/ 67/6
push /pʊʃ/ 65/6
put /pʊt/ 66/15
†pyjamas /pə'dʒɑːməz/ 10/4
pylon /'paɪlɒn/ 37/5
pyramid /'pɪrəmɪd/ 68/22

quantity /'kwɒntɪtɪ/ 72–73
quarter /'kwɔːtə(r)/ 69/14; 70/7, 9
quay /kiː/ 42/5
queen /kwiːn/ 52/7, 12

rabbit /'ræbɪt/ 56/20
race-horse /'reɪs hɔːs/ 46/2
rack /ræk/ 28/13; 30/10; 41/9
racket /'rækɪt/ 48/27
radiator /'reɪdɪeɪtə(r)/ 38/33
'radiator grill 38/27
radio /'reɪdɪəʊ/ 29/22; 38/25
radius /'reɪdɪəs/ 68/17
rafter /'rɑːftə(r)/ 23/3
rail /reɪl/ 33/21
railway-line /'reɪlweɪ laɪn/ 41/24
‡train /reɪn/ 27/3
raincoat 11/12
'raindrop 27/4
rat /ræt/ 56/22
rattle /'rætl/ 32/30
razor /'reɪzə(r)/ 33/12
'razor-blade 33/13
read /riːd/ 65/7
reading /'riːdɪŋ/ 52/C

rear /rɪə(r)/ 38/1; 40/30
receipt /rɪ'siːt/ 20/23
receiver /rɪ'siːvə(r)/ 28/26
record /'rekɔːd/ 29/20
'record-player 29/11
‡recreation /ˌrekrɪ'eɪʃn/ 46–52
rectangle /'rektæŋgl/ 68/D
red /red/ 79
Red Sea /ˌred 'siː/ 6/25
reel /riːl/ 53/8; 73/9
referee /ˌrefə'riː/ 46/10; 47/3
refinery /rɪ'faɪnərɪ/ 37/13
reflector /rɪ'flektə(r)/ 40/20
refrigerator /rɪ'frɪdʒəreɪtə(r)/ 30/5
reindeer /'reɪndɪə(r)/ 56/11
†reins /reɪnz/ 40/24; 46/4
relationship /rɪ'leɪʃnʃɪp/ 71
reptile /'reptaɪl/ 59/A
reservoir /'rezəvwɑː(r)/ 37/1
restaurant /'restərɒnt/ 51
revolver /rɪ'vɒlvə(r)/ 45/12
rhinoceros /raɪ'nɒsərəs/ 57/25
rib /rɪb/ 8/5
ribbon /'rɪbn/ 53/24
‡rice /raɪs/ 63/7
ride /raɪd/ 65/8
rifle /'raɪfl/ 45/2
rig /rɪg/ 37/11
right /raɪt/ 47/16, 19, 23, 24
'right angle 68/14
rind /raɪnd/ 61/18
ring /rɪŋ/ 12/18; 30/4; 46/13
river /'rɪvə(r)/ 7/F; 34/12
road /rəʊd/ 15/34; 34/18
robe /rəʊb/ 16/24
rock /rɒk/ 35/29
rocket /'rɒkɪt/ 44/10
Rockies /'rɒkɪz/ 7/36
rod /rɒd/ 48/19
roll /rəʊl/ 52/24; 73/12
rolling-pin /'rəʊlɪŋ pɪn/ 30/18
roof /ruːf/ 26/1
rook /rʊk/ 52/11
room /rʊm/ 29; 32; 33; 41/18
root /ruːt/ 63/11
rope /rəʊp/ 46/14
rose /rəʊz/ 62/19
rostrum /'rɒstrəm/ 49/13
rotor /'rəʊtə(r)/ 44/16
rough /rʌf/ 75/4, 5
round /raʊnd/ 76/6
'roundabout 39/4
row /rəʊ/ 72/14
rowing-boat /'rəʊɪŋ bəʊt/ 43/6
rubber /'rʌbə(r)/ 18/14
rubbish-bin /'rʌbɪʃ bɪn/ 30/9
rucksack /'rʌksæk/ 35/4
Rugby /'rʌgbɪ/ 46/H
rug /rʌg/ 28/12; 32/16
ruler /'ruːlə(r)/ 18/10
run /rʌn/ 65/9
rung /rʌŋ/ 23/6
runway /'rʌnweɪ/ 44/19

sack /sæk/ 67/13
sad /sæd/ 74/11
saddle /'sædl/ 40/7; 46/3
'saddlebag 40/8
safe /seɪf/ 67/20
safety-belt /'seɪftɪ belt/ 38/24
'safety-pin 53/10
Sahara /sə'hɑːrə/ 7/41
sail /seɪl/ 43/4; 65/10
sailor /'seɪlə(r)/ 55/15
salesman /'seɪlzmən/ 55/9
‡salmon /'sæmən/ 58/4
saloon /sə'luːn/ 38/37
salt /sɔːlt/ 51/27
‡sand /sænd/ 23/15; 35/22
sandal /'sændl/ 13/7
'sandcastle 35/23
'sandpaper 24/3
satchel /'sætʃl/ 18/19
satellite /'sætəlaɪt/ 4/18
Saturday /'sætədɪ/ 80
saucepan /'sɔːspən/ 30/12
saucer /'sɔːsə(r)/ 29/31
sausage /'sɒsɪdʒ/ 20/12
saw /sɔː/ 25/17
saxophone /'sæksəfəʊn/ 49/22
‡scaffolding /'skæfəldɪŋ/ 23/7
scale /skeɪl/ 58/9
scales /skeɪlz/ 19/1· 22/2; 30/17; 33/22

scarecrow /'skeəkrəʊ/ 36/13
scarf /skɑ:f/ 11/19; 13/13
‡scent /sent/ 12/16
school /sku:l/ 18
'schoolbag 18/9
'schoolgirl 18/8
science /'saɪəns/ 19
†scissors /'sɪzəz/ 53/26
scooter /'sku:tə(r)/ 40/29
scorpion /'skɔ:pɪən/ 58/27
scourer /'skaʊrə(r)/ 30/26
‡scouring powder /'skaʊrɪŋ paʊdə(r)/ 31/9
screen /skri:n/ 29/18; 50/18; 52/27
screw /skru:/ 25/9
screwdriver /'skru:draɪvə(r)/ 24/7
scrubbing-brush /'skrʌbɪŋ brʌʃ/ 31/10
sea /si:/ 6–7/C; 35/31
'sea-front 35/9
'seagull 60/21
seal /si:l/ 22/18; 57/9
‡sealing-wax /'si:lɪŋ wæks/ 22/19
seam /si:m/ 53/3
‡seaside 35/B
seat /si:t/ 38/23; 40/31; 41/8; 50/20
'seat-belt 38/24
'sea-'wall 35/10
‡seaweed /'si:wi:d/ 35/37
second /'sekənd/ 70/3; 80
secretary /'sekrətrɪ/ 21/22
sector /'sektə(r)/ 68/21
seed /si:d/ 62/28
segment /'segmənt/ 61/17
September /sep'tembə(r)/ 80
server /'sɜ:və(r)/ 48/25
service /'sɜ:vɪs/ 17; 48/26
'service-station 39/7
serviette /,sɜ:vɪ'et/ 51/31
set /set/ 50/4
'set-square 18/16
settee /se'ti:/ 29/21
seven /'sevn/ 80
seventeen /,sevn'ti:n/ 80
seventh /'sevnθ/ 80
seventy /'sevntɪ/ 80
sew /səʊ/ 65/11
sewing /'səʊɪŋ/ 53
'sewing-machine 53/1
shallow /'ʃæləʊ/ 74/6
shape /ʃeɪp/ 68
shark /ʃɑ:k/ 58/1
sharp /ʃɑ:p/ 74/2
shaving-brush /'ʃeɪvɪŋ brʌʃ/ 33/14
shawl /ʃɔ:l/ 12/5
she /ʃi:/ 79
†shears /ʃɪəz/ 24/11
shed /ʃed/ 26/20; 27/26
‡sheep /ʃi:p/ 36/29
'sheepdog 36/28
sheet /ʃi:t/ 21/10; 32/5; 49/12
shelf /ʃelf/ 20/15; 30/16
shell /ʃel/ 35/27; 45/7; 58/14; 59/5
shepherd /'ʃepəd/ 36/26
ship /ʃɪp/ 42/7
shirt /ʃɜ:t/ 11/1
shoe /ʃu:/ 10/9; 11/8; 13/12
shoelace /'ʃu:leɪs/ 11/9
shoot /ʃu:t/ 65/12
shop /ʃɒp/ 15/22
'shop-assistant 20/8
'shopping basket 67/10
,shop-'window 15/23; 20/1
short /ʃɔ:t/ 74/16
†shorts /ʃɔ:ts/ 10/12
shoulder /'ʃəʊldə(r)/ 8/13
'shoulder-blade 8/3
shovel /'ʃʌvl/ 23/13
shower /'ʃaʊə(r)/ 33/4
shrub /ʃrʌb/ 27/22
shut /ʃʌt/ 65/13; 74/4
shutter /'ʃʌtə(r)/ 26/12
side /saɪd/ 68/13; 69/5
siding /'saɪdɪŋ/ 41/30
sieve /sɪv/ 30/30
signal /'sɪgnl/ 41/27
'signal-box 41/23
'signalman 41/22
signpost /'saɪnpəʊst/ 14/8
sill /sɪl/ 26/11
sing /sɪŋ/ 65/14
singer /'sɪŋə(r)/ 49/24
sink /sɪŋk/ 30/7
sister /'sɪstə(r)/ 71/5
sister-in-law /'sɪstər ɪn lɔ:/ 71/8

sit /sɪt/ 65/15
site /saɪt/ 23
sitting-room /'sɪtɪŋ rʊm/ 29
six /sɪks/ 80
sixteen /,sɪks'ti:n/ 80
sixth /sɪksθ/ 80
sixty /'sɪkstɪ/ 80
skate /skeɪt/ 47/31
skater /'skeɪtə(r)/ 47/30
skeleton /'skelɪtn/ 8/A
ski /ski:/ 47/26
skier /'ski:ə(r)/ 47/25
‡skin /skɪn/ 61/6
skip /skɪp/ 23/24
'ski-pole 47/27
skirt /skɜ:t/ 13/2
'ski-stick 47/27
skull /skʌl/ 8/1
sky /skaɪ/ 27/10
sleep /sli:p/ 66/19
sleeper /'sli:pə(r)/ 41/25
'sleeping-bag /'sli:pɪŋ bæg/ 35/3
'sleeping suit 32/27
sleeve /sli:v/ 11/7
slice /slaɪs/ 73/8
slide /slaɪd/ 19/11; 49/21; 52/30
'slide-projector 52/29
'slide-rule 18/20
sling /slɪŋ/ 17/23
slip /slɪp/ 12/2; 32/4
slipper /'slɪpə(r)/ 10/5; 12/7
slow /sləʊ/ 74/9
slug /slʌg/ 58/19
small /smɔ:l/ 74/1
smile /smaɪl/ 65/16
‡smoke /sməʊk/ 17/12
smooth /smu:ð/ 75/5
snail /sneɪl/ 58/13
snake /sneɪk/ 59/6
snapshot /'snæpʃɒt/ 52/22
snorkel /'snɔ:kl/ 35/16
snout /snaʊt/ 56/4
‡snow /snəʊ/ 27/5
snowball 27/6
snowman 27/7
‡soap /səʊp/ 33/25
‡soap powder /'səʊp paʊdə(r)/ 31/18
‡soccer /'sɒkə(r)/ 47/A
sock /sɒk/ 10/14; 13/3
socket /'sɒkɪt/ 31/16
sofa /'səʊfə/ 29/21
soft /sɒft/ 51/13; 74/13; 75/13
soldier /'səʊldʒə(r)/ 45/1; 55/12
sole /səʊl/ 9/40; 11/10
solid /'sɒlɪd/ 68/G; 75/14
son /sʌn/ 71/3
son-in-law /'sʌn ɪn lɔ:/ 71/7
south /saʊθ/ 5/C
,South ,China 'Sea 7/31
southeast /,saʊθ'i:st/ 5/C
Southern /'sʌðən/ 6/14
,South 'Pole 5/7
southwest /,saʊθ'west/ 5/C
‡space /speɪs/ 4/A
'space-capsule 4/19
'spacesuit 4/21
‡'space-travel 4/C
spade /speɪd/ 24/9; 35/25; 52/14
spanner /'spænə(r)/ 24/13
sparking-plug /'spɑ:kɪŋ plʌg/ 38/35
sparrow /'spærəʊ/ 60/28
speedometer /spɪ'dɒmɪtə(r)/ 38/16
spider /'spaɪdə(r)/ 58/25
spin /spɪn/ 66/16
spine /spaɪn/ 8/6; 52/18
spiral /'spaɪərəl/ 68/1
spoke /spəʊk/ 40/12
sponge /spʌndʒ/ 33/24
spoon /spu:n/ 17/31; 29/27
sport /spɔ:t/ 46–48
sportscar /'spɔ:tskɑ:(r)/ 39/18
spot /spɒt/ 47/11
spotlight 50/7
spout /spaʊt/ 29/34
square /skweə(r)/ 68/C
squirrel /'skwɪrəl/ 56/19
stadium /'steɪdɪəm/ 47/B
stage /steɪdʒ/ 50/1
stair /steə(r)/ 28/16
staircase 28/17
stalk /stɔ:k/ 61/2; 62/2
stall /stɔ:l/ 14/3
stalls /stɔ:lz/ 50/11

stamp /stæmp/ 22/9
stand /stænd/ 47/5; 52/28; 65/17
staple /'steɪpl/ 21/8
stapler /'steɪplə(r)/ 21/7
star /stɑ:(r)/ 4/5
starter /'stɑ:tə(r)/ 40/36
station /'steɪʃn/ 41/13
steering-wheel /'stɪərɪŋ wi:l/ 38/17
stem /stem/ 62/23
stethoscope /'steθəskəʊp/ 17/22
stick /stɪk/ 46/18; 47/27
stir /stɜ:(r)/ 65/18
stirrup /'stɪrəp/ 46/7
stitch /stɪtʃ/ 53/17
stomach /'stʌmək/ 8/17
stone /stəʊn/ 61/8, 20
stool /stu:l/ 19/8; 32/11; 49/18; 51/20
storage tank /'stɔ:rɪdʒ tæŋk/ 37/14
storm-cloud /'stɔ:m klaʊd/ 27/2
stove /stəʊv/ 30/1; 35/5
straight /streɪt/ 42/5; 74/5
strainer /'streɪnə(r)/ 30/30
straw /strɔ:/ 51/12
strawberry /'strɔ:brɪ/ 61/21
stream /stri:m/ 34/7
street /stri:t/ 15/34
stress /stres/ 81
stretcher /'stretʃə(r)/ 17/32
striker /'straɪkə(r)/ 47/20–24
‡string /strɪŋ/ 22/21; 49/5; 72/8
strong /strɒŋ/ 75/6
stumps /stʌmps/ 48/9
submarine /,sʌbmə'ri:n/ 45/19
sugar-bowl /'ʃʊgə bəʊl/ 29/39
‡sugar-cane /'ʃʊgə keɪn/ 63/9
suit /su:t/ 11/6; 46/23
'suitcase 67/17
sun /sʌn/ 4/8; 27/9
sunbather 35/13
Sunday /'sʌndɪ/ 80
‡†'sunfish 58/15
'sunflower 62/27
'sunshade 35/12
supermarket /'su:pəmɑ:kɪt/ 20
‡surf sɜ:f/ 35/32
swallow /'swɒləʊ/ 60/22
swan /swɒn/ 60/17
swarm /swɔ:m/ 72/16
sweater /'swetə(r)/ 13/5
sweep /swi:p/ 65/19
swim /swɪm/ 65/20
swimming /'swɪmɪŋ/
'swimming-costume 35/36
'swimming trunks 35/20
switch /swɪtʃ/ 28/23; 31/17
'switchboard 21/15
‡†swordfish /'sɔ:dfɪʃ/ 58/3
symbol /'sɪmbl/ 81

T-shirt /'ti: ʃɜ:t/ 10/11
table /teɪbl/ 29/19, 23; 32/9, 10; 46/23
'table-cloth 51/30
'table-mat 29/25
tablet /'tæblɪt/ 73/3
‡'table-tennis 46/E
tail /teɪl/ 44/13; 56/23; 58/7
tank /tæŋk/ 37/14; 45/8; 67/21
tankard /'tæŋkəd/ 51/14
tanker /'tæŋkə(r)/ 39/19; 43/18
tap /tæp/ 33/2, 3
tape /teɪp/ 53/2
'tape-measure 53/25
Tasman Sea /,tæzmən 'si:/ 6/30
taxi /'tæksɪ/ 14/5
tea /ti:/ 63/8
teacher /'ti:tʃə(r)/ 18/1; 55/11
team /ti:m/ 72/15
teapot 29/36
tear /teə(r)/ 65/21
teat /ti:t/ 32/34
'tea-towel 30/32
teddy-bear /'tedɪ beə(r)/ 32/29
telegram /'telɪgræm/ 22/16
telephone /'telɪfəʊn/ 21/2; 28/25
'telephone-box 15/31
'telephone directory 28/29
television /'telɪvɪʒn/ 29/17, 18
temperature /'temprətʃə(r)/ 70/C
temple /'templ/ 9/7
ten /ten/ 80
tennis /'tenɪs/ 46/E; 48/D
'tennis-ball 48/28
'tennis-shoe 10/15

tent /tent/ 35/1
tentacle /'tentəkl/ 58/24
tenth /tenθ/ 80
test-tube /'test tju:b/ 19/22
text /tekst/ 52/21
'textbook 18/19
that /ðæt/ 79
theatre /'θɪətə(r)/ 50/8
their /ðeə(r)/ 79
theirs /ðeəz/ 79
them /ðəm, ðem/ 79
there /ðeə(r)/ 79
thermometer /θə'mɒmɪtə(r)/ 17/28; 70/12
thermos flask /'θɜːməs flɑːsk/ 67/9
these ðiːz/ 79
they /ðeɪ/ 79
thick /θɪk/ 75/15
thigh /θaɪ/ 8/33
thimble /'θɪmbl/ 53/5
thin /θɪn/ 74/10; 75/15
third /θɜːd/ 69/13; 80
thirteen /ˌθɜː'tiːn/ 80
thirty /'θɜːtɪ/ 80
this /ðɪs/ 79
those /ðəʊz/ 79
thousand /'θaʊznd/ 80
thread /θred/ 25/10
three /θriː/ 80
throat θrəʊt/ 8/12
throttle /'θrɒtl/ 40/32
through /θruː/ 76/2
throw /θrəʊ/ 66/9
thumb /θʌm/ 8/29
thunder-cloud /'θʌndə klaʊd/ 27/2
Thursday /'θɜːzdɪ/ 80
ticket /'tɪkɪt/ 41/7
'ticket-collector 41/16
'ticket-inspector 41/16
'ticket-office 41/14
tidy /'taɪdɪ/ 75/7
tie /taɪ/ 11/4; 65/23
tiger /'taɪgə(r)/ 57/19
tight /taɪt/ 75/16
†tights /taɪts/ 12/4
tile /taɪl/ 23/4
time /taɪm/ 70/A; 80
'timetable 18/22; 41/15
tin /tɪn/ 30/19, 22
tinned food /ˌtɪnd 'fuːd/ 20/16
'tin-opener 30/21
tipper-truck /'tɪpə trʌk/ 23/22
tissue /'tɪʃuː/ 32/22
to /tə, tuː/ 77/4
toboggan /tə'bɒgən/ 47/29
tobogganist /tə'bɒgənɪst/ 47/28
toe /təʊ/ 9/41
toilet /'tɔɪlɪt/ 33/7
‡'toilet-paper 33/9
'toilet-roll 33/9
tomato /tə'mɑːtəʊ/ 62/15
tongue /tʌŋ/ 9/14; 59/8
tool /tuːl/ 25
tooth /tuːθ/ 9/12
'toothbrush 33/15
'toothmug 33/16
‡'toothpaste 33/19
top /tɒp/ 51/2; 69/1
torch /tɔːtʃ/ 16/9
torpedo /tɔː'piːdəʊ/ 45/17
tortoise /'tɔːtəs/ 59/2
touch /tʌtʃ/ 65/22
'touch-line 47/12
towards /tə'wɔːdz/ 77/10
towel /'taʊəl/ 33/20; 35/14
'towel-rail 33/21
town /taʊn/ 14–15
tractor /'træktə(r)/ 36/18
traffic-light /'træfɪk laɪt/ 14/7
trailer /'treɪlə(r)/ 39/21
train /treɪn/ 41
transporter /træn'spɔːtə(r)/ 39/12
travel /'trævl/ 38–44
trawler /'trɔːlə(r)/ 43/17
tray /treɪ/ 30/14
tree /triː/ 27/11; 34/15; 63/10
triangle /'traɪæŋgl/ 68/B
trigger /'trɪgə(r)/ 45/13
tripod /'traɪpɒd/ 19/13
trombone /trɒm'bəʊn/ 49/20
Tropic /'trɒpɪk/ 5/3, 5
†trousers /'traʊzəz/ 11/17; 13/6
trowel /'traʊəl/ 23/17; 24/12
truck /trʌk/ 23/22; 41/28
trumpet /'trʌmpɪt/ 49/19

truncheon /'trʌntʃən/ 16/7
trunk /trʌŋk/ 27/12; 57/22; 63/12; 67/12
†trunks /trʌŋks/ 35/20
T-shirt /'tiː ʃɜːt/ 10/11
tube /tjuːb/ 19/22; 33/19; 73/13
tubing /'tjuːbɪŋ/ 19/14
Tuesday /'tjuːzdɪ/ 80
tug /tʌg/ 42/19
tulip /'tjuːlɪp/ 62/22
tummy /'tʌmɪ/ 8/17
turkey /'tɜːkɪ/ 60/16
turn /tɜːn/ 66/10
'turn-up 11/18
turtle /'tɜːtl/ 59/4
tusk /tʌsk/ 57/23
‡TV /ˌtiː 'viː/ 29/17
twelve /twelv/ 80
twentieth /'twentɪəθ/ 80
twenty /'twentɪ/ 80
ˌtwenty-'one 80
twig /twɪg/ 27/14; 63/14
two /tuː/ 80
type /taɪp/ 66/21
typewriter /'taɪpraɪtə(r)/ 21/21
typist /'taɪpɪst/ 21/22; 54/9
tyre /'taɪə(r)/ 38/8; 40/11

ugly /'ʌglɪ/ 75/9
umbrella /ʌm'brelə/ 11/24; 13/17
umpire /'ʌmpaɪə(r)/ 48/16
uncle /'ʌŋkl/ 71/10
under /'ʌndə(r)/ 76/17
ˌunder'neath 76/17
underpass 39/3
uniform /'juːnɪfɔːm/ 16/3
universe /'juːnɪvɜːs/ 4
untidy /ʌn'taɪdɪ/ 75/7
up /ʌp/ 76/5
ˌup'stairs 28/20
Urals /'jʊərəlz/ 7/39
urn /ɜːn/ 67/2
us /əs, ʌs/ 79
usherette /ˌʌʃə'ret/ 50/19

vacuum-cleaner /'vækjʊəm kliːnə(r)/ 31/1
vacuum-flask /'vækjʊəm flɑːsk/ 67/9
valley /'vælɪ/ 34/16
valve /vælv/ 40/13
van /væn/ 14/14; 39/22
vase /vɑːz/ 29/14
vegetable /'vedʒtəbl/ 20/18; 62
'vegetable-rack 30/10
vein /veɪn/ 9/29
verb /vɜːb/ 64–66
vest /vest/ 10/1
vice /vaɪs/ 24/8
village /'vɪlɪdʒ/ 34/16
vine /vaɪn/ 61/13
viola /vɪ'əʊlə/ 49/7
violin /ˌvaɪə'lɪn/ 49/4
vowel /'vaʊəl/ 81
vulture /'vʌltʃə(r)/ 60/10

waggon /'wægən/ 41/28
waist /weɪst/ 8/16
waistcoat /'weɪskəʊt/ 11/5
waiter /'weɪtə(r)/ 51/21
'waiting-room /'weɪtɪŋ rʊm/ 41/18
waitress /'weɪtrəs/ 54/11
walk /wɔːk/ 65/24
wall /wɔːl/ 26/3; 29/2
wallet /'wɒlɪt/ 67/16
walnut /'wɔːlnʌt/ 61/27
ward /wɔːd/ 17/C
warder /'wɔːdə(r)/ 16/13
wardrobe /'wɔːdrəʊb/ 32/14
warehouse /'weəhaʊs/ 42/3
warship /'wɔːʃɪp/ 45/16
wash /wɒʃ/ 65/25
'wash-basin 33/11
washer /'wɒʃə(r)/ 25/12
‡washing /'wɒʃɪŋ/ 27/29
'washing-line 27/29
'washing-machine 31/4
ˌwashing-'up brush 30/27
‡ˌwashing-'up liquid 30/28
wasp /wɒsp/ 59/22
wastepaper basket /ˌweɪst 'peɪpə bɑːskɪt/ 21/13
'waste-pipe 23/9
watch /wɒtʃ/ 11/21
'watch-strap 11/22
water /'wɔːtə(r)/ 42–43
'waterfall 34/4
'watering-can /'wɔːtərɪŋ kæn/ 27/23

'waterlily 62/26
wave /weɪv/ 35/33; 66/1
wavy /'weɪvɪ/ 68/7
wax /wæks/ 22/19
we /wiː/ 79
weak /wiːk/ 75/6
‡weather /'weðə(r)/ 27
web /web/ 58/26
webbed /webd/ 60/9
Wednesday /'wenzdɪ/ 80
week /wiːk/ 80
weep /wiːp/ 64/7
weight /weɪt/ 19/3; 80
wellington /'welɪŋtən/ 10/10
west /west/ 5/C
wet /wet/ 74/7
whale /weɪl/ 57/1
wharf /wɔːf/ 42/5
what /wɒt/ 79
‡wheat /wiːt/ 36/14; 63/2
wheel /wiːl/ 40/9
'wheelbarrow 27/27
where /weə(r)/ 79
which /wɪtʃ/ 79
whip /wɪp/ 40/25
whisker /'wɪskə(r)/ 56/21
whistle /'wɪsl/ 41/12; 47/4
white /waɪt/ 79
who /huː/ 79
whose /huːz/ 79
wicket /'wɪkɪt/ 48/9, 11
wide /waɪd/ 75/1
width /wɪdθ/ 69/8
wife /waɪf/ 71/1
wig /wɪg/ 16/25
willow /'wɪləʊ/ 63/24
wind /waɪnd/ 66/3
'windbreak 35/18
windlass /'wɪndləs/ 42/16
window /'wɪndəʊ/ 15/23; 26/8
'window-box 26/13
'window-frame 26/9
'window-ledge 26/11
'window-pane 26/10
'window-sill 26/11
'windpipe 9/22
'windscreen 38/10
'windscreen-wiper 38/11
wine /waɪn/ 51/24
wing /wɪŋ/ 44/11; 60/23
wings /wɪŋz/ 50/5
†winter sports /ˌwɪntə 'spɔːts/ 47/D
witness /'wɪtnɪs/ 16/19
'witness-box 16/18
wolf /wʊlf/ 57/11
woman /'wʊmən/ 12–13
wood /wʊd/ 34/8
‡wool /wʊl/ 53/19
workbench /'wɜːkbentʃ/ 24/1
workman /'wɜːkmən/ 23/14
workshop /'wɜːkʃɒp/ 24
world /wɜːld/ 5–7
worm /wɜːm/ 58/21
wrench /rentʃ/ 24/6
wrestler /'reslə(r)/ 46/22
‡wrestling /'reslɪŋ/ 46/F
wrist /rɪst/ 8/25
write /raɪt/ 66/2
‡'writing-paper /'raɪtɪŋ peɪpə(r)/ 22/12

x-ray /ˌeks 'reɪ/ 17/24

yacht /jɒt/ 43/1
Yangtze /'jæŋtsɪ/ 7/55
year /jɜː(r)/ 80
yellow /'jeləʊ/ 79
Yellow River /jeləʊ 'rɪvə(r)/ 7/54
you /jə, juː/ 79
young /jʌŋ/ 75/2
your /jɔː(r)/ 79
yours /jɔːz/ 79

zebra /'ziːbrə/ 57/24
zero /'zɪərəʊ/ 80
zig-zag /'zɪg zæg/ 68/6
zip /zɪp/ 53/22
'zip-fastener 53/22
zipper /'zɪpə(r)/ 53/22

Jennifer Worth trained as a nurse at the Royal Berkshire Hospital, Reading, and was later ward sister at the Elizabeth Garrett Anderson Hospital in London, then the Marie Curie Hospital, also in London. Music had always been her passion, and in 1973 she left nursing in order to study music intensively, teaching piano and singing for about twenty-five years. Jennifer died in May 2011 after a short illness, leaving her husband Philip, two daughters and three grandchildren. Her books have all been bestsellers.

By Jennifer Worth

Eczema and Food Allergy
Call the Midwife
Shadows of the Workhouse
Farewell to the East End
In the Midst of Life
Call the Midwife: Illustrated Edition